US-Iran relations

OCT 0 8 2018

VIEWPOINTS ON
MODERN WORLD HISTORY

US–Iran Relations

Other Books of Related Interest

At Issue Series

Does the World Hate the U.S.?
Foreign Oil Dependence
Is Iran a Threat to Global Security?
What Role Should the U.S. Play in the Middle East?

Current Controversies Series

Iran
The Arms Trade
The Middle East

Opposing Viewpoints Series

America's Global Influence
Iran
Iraq
Islamic Militancy
The Arab Spring
The Middle East Peace Process

VIEWPOINTS ON
MODERN WORLD HISTORY

US–Iran Relations

Avery Elizabeth Hurt, Book Editor

GREENHAVEN
PUBLISHING

Published in 2018 by Greenhaven Publishing, LLC
353 3rd Avenue, Suite 255, New York, NY 10010

Articles in Greenhaven Publishing anthologies are often edited for length to meet page
requirements. In addition, original titles of these works are changed to clearly present
the main thesis and to explicitly indicate the author's opinion. Every effort is made to
ensure that Greenhaven Publishing accurately reflects the original intent of the authors.
Every effort has been made to trace the owners of the copyrighted material.

Cover image: ATTA KENARE/AFP/Getty Images.

Library of Congress Cataloging-in-Publication Data

Names: Hurt, Avery Elizabeth, editor.
Title: U.S.-Iran relations / Avery Elizabeth Hurt, book editor.
Description: First edition. | New York : Greenhaven Publishing, [2018] | Series: Viewpoints on
modern world history | Includes bibliographical references and index. | Audience: Grades 9–12.
Identifiers: LCCN 2017027357 | ISBN 9781534501355 (library bound)
Subjects: LCSH: United States—Relations—Iran—Juvenile literature. | Iran—Relations—United
State—Juvenile literature. | Iran—Politics and government—20th century—Juvenile literature.
Classification: LCC E183.8.I55 U5745 2018 | DDC 327.73055--dc23
LC record available at https://lccn.loc.gov/2017027357

Manufactured in the United States of America

Website: http://greenhavenpublishing.com

Contents

of debating the deal could benefit Israel and American
supporters of Israel.

Foreword

"The more we know about the past enables us to ask richer and more provocative questions about who we are today. We also must tell the next generation one of the great truths of history: that no past event was preordained. Every battle, every election, and revolution could have turned out differently at any point along the way, just as a person's own life can change unpredictably."

—David McCullough, American historian

History is punctuated by momentous events—turning points for the nations involved, with impacts felt far beyond their borders. Displaying the full range of human capabilities—from violence, greed, and ignorance to heroism, courage, and strength—they are nearly always complicated and multifaceted. Any student of history faces the challenge of grasping both the broader elements and the nuances of world-changing events, such as wars, social movements, and environmental disasters. Textbooks offer only so much help, burdened as they are by constraints of length and single-perspective narratives. True understanding of history's significant events comes from exposure to a variety of perspectives from the people involved intimately, as well as those observing from a distance of miles or years.

Viewpoints on Modern World History examines global events from the twentieth century onward, presenting analysis and observation from numerous vantage points. The series offers high school, early college level, and general interest readers a thematically arranged anthology of previously published materials that address a major historical event or period. Each volume opens with background information on the event, presents the controversies surrounding the event, and concludes with the implications and legacy of the event. By providing a variety of perspectives, this series can be used to inform debate, help develop critical-thinking skills, increase global awareness, and enhance an understanding of international viewpoints on history.

Material in each volume is selected from a diverse range of sources. Articles taken from these sources are carefully edited and introduced to provide context and background.

Each volume in the Viewpoints on Modern World History series also includes:

- An annotated **table of contents** that provides a brief summary of each essay in the volume
- An **introduction** specific to the volume topic
- A **chapter preface** setting up the chapter content and providing historical context
- For each viewpoint, a brief **introduction** that has notes about the author and source of the viewpoint and provides a summary of its main points
- Informational **sidebars** that explore the lives of key individuals, give background on historical events, or explain scientific or technical concepts
- A **chronology** of dates important to the period
- A **bibliography** of additional books, periodicals, and websites for further research
- A **subject index** that offers links to people, places, and events cited in the text

Viewpoints on Modern World History is designed for a broad spectrum of readers who want to learn more about not only history but also current events, political science, government, international relations, and sociology. This includes students doing research for class assignments or debates, teachers and faculty seeking to supplement course materials, and others wanting to improve their understanding of history. The volumes in this series are designed to illuminate a complicated event, to spark debate, and to show the human perspective behind the world's most significant happenings of recent decades.

Introduction

"Relations between the United States and Iran have been complicated and edgy as long as anyone can remember."

—Douglas Little, professor of history
and international relations

In the United States, we think something a couple of hundred years old is ancient, but when it comes to ancient, Iran is the real deal. The history of the United States reaches back fewer than two-and-a-half centuries. The history and culture of Iran, on the other hand, go back two and a half millennia. What is now Iran was once known as Persia (Iran changed its name in 1935). The Persian Empire is perhaps best known in the West for having brought the world "algebra" (and perhaps carpets), but it is also the source of incredible poetry, music, and architecture that is still appreciated today. After the Muslim conquest of the Middle East (632–700 CE), the Persian Empire adopted the Islamic faith. Today virtually all Iranians are Muslims, and over a third of the world's Muslims live in Iran.

The United States didn't pay much attention to Iran until after the second World War, when vast oil reserves were discovered there. In 1953, the United States and Britain helped to overthrow Iran's prime minister and replace him with a monarch who was friendly to the West. In this arrangement, the United States and Britain got oil and Iran got military aid, allowing the country to build a formidable military, becoming one of the most powerful military powers in the region. During these years, Iran was a very secular and westernized nation. Then in 1979, a revolution in Iran overthrew the U.S.-backed hereditary monarch, known as the Shah, and replaced him with a spiritual leader, the Ayatollah. In this new form of government, an Islamic Republic, a popularly elected president was in charge of the government, but the Ayatollah was the most powerful official and was known as the Supreme Leader. This new government was virulently anti-American. Since that time, the relationship between the two countries has been difficult at best, and at times quite poisonous, particularly after a group of revolutionaries took a group of Americans hostage shortly after the 1979 revolution.

After the hostage situation was resolved (more than a year later), the two countries have engaged in a delicate diplomatic dance that tries to keep the peace while taking into account the complex alliances and enmities of the region, the economic interests of the two nations, and, of course, the fact that, as you shall see in chapter three, after so many years of trade and business relations, many Americans and many Iranians have close family ties with one another and scientists from Iran and the United States regularly collaborate.

In recent years, the United States has worked with Iran to come to an agreement to prevent Iran from developing nuclear weapons capabilities. This required very delicate negotiations over several years. The lasting effects of these and other negotiations remain to be seen, as the Trump administration sends conflicting and often hostile signals to Iran while the people of Iran welcome and embrace modernization and engagement—though the clerics most certainly do not.

After the articles in this collection were published, Iran had another presidential election. In the spring of 2017, just as this book was being prepared, Hassan Rouhani won reelection as Iran's president. He earned 56 percent of the vote in an election that saw 73 percent turnout. (For comparison, turnout in the 2016 US presidential election was 58 percent.) While Rouhani's reelection is in part a reflection of the public's support for the nuclear deal, it could not have been the only factor, because all of the candidates vowed to continue the deal. As you read these articles you will notice that the main text of most discussions about Iran focus on nuclear weapons, terrorism, and tensions between Islam and the West. But ordinary Iranians are as concerned, if not more concerned, with the same kinds of issues that preoccupy Americans: environmental issues including climate change (and in the case of that desert nation, particularly water shortages), social concerns, and their future. But far and away the most important issue for Iranian voters is, much like their counterparts in the West, the economy.

Rouhani spoke to these concerns. He reached out to secular and reformist Iranians, promising to rid the government of corruption, end the suppression of dissent, and to modernize and open Iranian society once more. It is unclear how much support Rouhani will get from Washington for these reforms. The very day that Iranians were celebrating their election, US president Donald Trump was in Saudi Arabia giving a speech that excoriated Iran for supporting terrorism while letting Saudi Arabia completely off the hook (and completing a large arms deals with the Saudis as well).

However their (or our) leaders feel about it, Iranian voters made abundantly clear what they want: economic prosperity and engagement with the rest of the world—including the United States. It is a great opportunity for the United States and Iran—nations that one of the writers in this volume called "frenemies"—to attempt to heal old wounds and forge a new and peaceful relationship. But the challenges remain enormous. The Trump administration has been openly hostile to Iran, threatening years of delicate negotiations that attempted to reduce the risks of war. And the volatility of the Middle East continues to make attempts at peace anywhere in the region exceedingly complex.

It is far too soon to know how many of his campaign promises Iran's new president can deliver, how much power he will be able to wrest from the clerics, or how much cooperation he can expect from the Trump administration. But it is clear that Iran does not fit the stereotype many Americans have of it. In the following viewpoints, you will learn more about the history of Iran—going back more than 2,500 years—and how the relationship of Iran and the United States has developed over the last century and a half, and what the future between the two nations might look like. Some of the voices in this volume are optimistic about the relationship while others are more cautious. But one thing all agree on is that while U.S.-Iran relations are and have never been easy, the relationship has always seemed worth working for.

The History of US- Iran Relations

Preface

The problems between the United States and Iran have their roots in a historical relationship that goes back many, many years. It has been a vexed relationship from the beginning of the twentieth century, when Americans first began involving themselves in Iranian affairs, to the Iran hostage crisis in 1979 to today's attempts to ease nuclear tensions between the two nations. Throughout the years, the United States has both interfered in Iran's government (by backing a coup to overthrow a legitimately elected government) and negotiated with it. US leaders have worked to keep relations smooth in the interest of protecting Western interests in Iranian oil and antagonized Iran in matters social and religious. Meanwhile, the citizens of the two nations have had an ambivalent relationship as well. While most ordinary Iranians and ordinary Americans think well enough of one another, as we shall see in the following viewpoints, lack of a free press in Iran and an excess of political propaganda in the United States has often stressed that relationship.

As you read the viewpoints in this chapter, you will notice a great deal of repetition of the history between the United States and Iran. Be on the lookout, however, for subtle changes in emphasis. Most experts agree on the general outlines of how the relation between the two nations has evolved over time and the key events that influenced this evolution. However, the factors that led to conflicts and the way those conflicts have been addressed are seen in slightly different ways from viewpoint to viewpoint.

While most of the pieces in this chapter focus on the careful diplomatic dance of the two governments, you will also find a great deal of information about Iranian culture and the Iranian people. Keep in mind as you read that this section covers the history of U.S.-Iran relations only up to the early twenty-first century, when the Iran nuclear deal was being negotiated.

The United States and Iran Have Always Had a Complex Relationship

Douglas Little

In this viewpoint, the author goes into detail about how relations between the United States and Iran have developed over the years, beginning at the outset of the twentieth century. Though many Americans have been concerned recently about the precarious relationship between the two countries, in this viewpoint we learn that relations between the two countries have long been dicey. Douglas Little, professor of history and international relations at Clark University in Worcester, Massachusetts, is an author of a seminal book on the United States and the Middle East and an expert on radical Islam.

Editor's Note: For more than 100 years, the United States and Iran have engaged in an ambivalent relationship. Although the American and Iranian people have usually regarded each other as friends, their governments have frequently treated each other as enemies. Throughout the 20th century and into the 21st, America and Iran have butted heads over issues as diverse as oil, communism, radical Islam, and nuclear proliferation, often framing their mutual antagonism as a clash between civilization and barbarism. Yet with a new administration in Washington eager to improve U.S. relations in the Muslim world and with young men and women calling for democracy in the streets of Tehran, the old "frenemies" may find that they have more in common than they think.

"Frenemies: Iran and America since 1900," by Douglas Little, Origins, May 2011. Reprinted by Permission. This article was originally published in Origins: Current Events Historical Perspective http://origins.osu.edu/article/frenemies-iran-andamerica-1900

American eyes have been riveted on North Africa and the Middle East these past months. The popular protests that rocked Tunis, Cairo, and Tripoli, and so many other cities during the "Arab Spring" of 2011 evoked memories of the violent confrontation between Iranian dissidents and President Mahmoud Ahmadinejad's Islamist regime in the streets of Tehran eighteen months earlier.

As in Tunisia and Egypt, Facebook and Twitter helped spread the word in June 2009 that Iran was teetering on the brink of revolution, and as in Libya, the ruling elite cracked down instinctively with brutal force. Unlike Libya's Muammar Qaddafi, however, Ahmadinejad stopped short of unleashing the Iranian air force against his opponents.

Yet, some Americans nevertheless expected that Iran's recent quest for nuclear weapons, its support for Islamic radicals like Lebanon's Hezbollah, and its destabilizing influence on the geopolitics of the Persian Gulf would eventually require U.S. military intervention.

Speaking off the record, one of President Barack Obama's top advisers recently confirmed that the Tomahawk missiles that the U.S. Sixth Fleet launched against Libya were also intended to send a message to Iran.

In fact, relations between the United States and Iran have been complicated and edgy as long as anyone can remember.

America's initial diplomatic encounter with Iran, or Persia, as it was called a century ago, did not go well.

On 9 March 1904, Kurdish bandits robbed and murdered Benjamin Labaree, a 38-year-old American missionary, not far from Mount Ararat in the no man's land just inside Iran's border with Ottoman Turkey.

Outraged by what the U.S. ambassador labeled an act of "religious and race hatred," the State Department demanded that Shah Mozaffar al-Din arrest the killers, pay Labaree's family an indemnity of $50,000 in gold, and assure "the civilized world" that Iran would prevent such atrocities in the future. Although the Shah of Iran was insulted by Uncle Sam's impertinence, he had little choice but to accept the U.S. demands.

Over the following decades, time and again a constantly shifting cast of Iranian and American leaders would butt heads over issues as diverse as oil wells, religion, and atomic bombs.

Much has changed over the years, of course, but to a very great degree, the United States and Iran today still frame their mutual antagonism as a clash between civilization and barbarism, much as they did when Benjamin Labaree was gunned down in a mountain pass 500 miles northwest of Tehran in 1904.

Oil and the Fate of Modern Iran

At the dawn of the twentieth century, Americans would have recognized Iran as an important imperial buffer between Russia and India, twice the size of Texas and famous mainly for exporting Persian rugs.

Then in 1901, the British-owned Anglo-Persian Oil Company secured an exclusive concession from Shah Mozaffar al-Din and his Qajar dynasty. Seven years later, the firm discovered a huge pool of petroleum at Masjid al-Suleiman in southwestern Iran, and the future of that country was transformed.

After World War I erupted in 1914, Anglo-Persian would satisfy the Royal Navy's rapidly expanding appetite for diesel fuel by pumping oil from the world's largest refinery at Abadan, near the headwaters of the Persian Gulf.

Mozaffar al-Din's successors accepted the small but steady stream of royalties that flowed into their coffers until 1925, when Reza Khan, an Iranian cavalry officer, overthrew the Qajars, proclaimed himself Shah, and established the Pahlavi dynasty.

A hard-headed nationalist, Reza Shah tried unsuccessfully to seize control of the oilfields from the recently rechristened Anglo-Iranian Oil Company (AIOC) in 1932 and flirted with Nazi Germany later that decade in an ill-advised effort to counterbalance Britain's influence. Troubled by the specter of a Berlin-Tehran axis, Winston Churchill and Josef Stalin secretly agreed to depose Reza Shah in August 1941, replacing him with his 20-year-old son Mohammed Reza Pahlavi. They also announced that their two nations would jointly occupy Iran for the duration of World War II—Britain in the south and Russia in the north.

Fearing that Iran might be carved up into permanent spheres of influence, Washington quickly secured pledges that both London and Moscow would withdraw their troops six months after the war ended. Meanwhile, America's stock rose in the eyes of many Iranians as U.S. advisers helped the young Shah plan the economic infrastructure essential for postwar modernization and development.

British forces pulled out of Iran on schedule, but when the Soviets refused to honor the March 1946 deadline, President Harry S. Truman decided, as Secretary of State James Byrnes put it, "to give it to them with both barrels," censuring the Kremlin at the United Nations and making thinly veiled nuclear threats. Stalin finally withdrew the Red Army two months later, but only after receiving assurances from Iranian Prime Minister Ahmed Qavam that the Soviet Union would have access to oil fields in northern Iran.

The Spoils of Oil: the United States, Mossadegh, and the Cold War

As the Cold War heated up during the late 1940s, the Truman administration embraced Mohammed Reza Pahlavi as an important partner in the informal anti-Soviet alliance emerging in the Middle East. This partnership was complicated, however, by mounting Iranian resentment against Britain and AIOC, which exported millions of barrels of oil and made huge profits while paying Iran next to nothing.

In October 1949, Mohammed Mossadegh, a long-time critic of the Pahlavi dynasty who insisted that Iran had a right to control its own oil industry, founded the National Front, a broad coalition that included both middle-class moderates as well as firebrands from the left-wing Tudeh or "Workers" Party.

Mossadegh and his supporters soon held the balance of power in the Majlis, the Iranian parliament, where they called for AIOC to split its profits with Iran on a 50-50 basis, as other multinational oil firms operating in Venezuela and Saudi Arabia had recently agreed to do. Backed by the British government, AIOC refused even to consider such an option. On 15 March 1951, the Majlis responded with legislation nationalizing the Iranian petroleum industry.

Six weeks later, Mossadegh became prime minister and announced plans to wrest control of Iran's oil fields and refineries from Britain as soon as possible. American officials, who had urged the British to accept a last-minute profit-sharing compromise, were appalled. "Never have so few lost so much so stupidly and so fast," Dean Acheson, Truman's secretary of state, recalled long afterward.

When Mossadegh moved forward with the nationalization of AIOC, the British government pressed the Shah to overrule his prime minister, sought American support for an international embargo on Iranian oil, and secretly began to plan a coup d'état in Tehran.

The MI6, Britain's overseas intelligence service, had developed a covert network of contacts among Iranian politicians and military officers and was quite confident that Mossadegh could be deposed with little bloodshed, provided the United States had no objection.

The Central Intelligence Agency (CIA) maintained close ties with MI6 in Iran and was well aware that British intelligence was working closely with General Fazlollah Zahedi, Mossadegh's former interior minister, who was eager to overthrow his old boss. Neither the White House nor the State Department, however, was enamored of the MI6 plot, especially after Mossadegh learned most of the details in October 1952 and expelled Britain's diplomats and spooks from Iran.

Just two months before handing the keys to the Oval Office over to Dwight Eisenhower, Harry Truman insisted that all covert action in Tehran be put on hold. "We tried to get the block-headed British to have their oil company make a fair deal with Iran," Truman complained privately, but "no, no, they could not do that."

President Eisenhower and his top advisers regarded the crisis in Iran very differently from their predecessors. Ike's secretary of state, John Foster Dulles, was a rabid anti-communist who dismissed Mohammed Mossadegh as a Russian stooge and who saw the Tudeh Party as the entering wedge for a Kremlin takeover in Tehran. Allen Dulles, the new CIA director and John Foster's younger brother, was an avid proponent of covert action with close ties to Britain's MI6 and had few qualms about meddling in the internal affairs of Iran or any other nation deemed vulnerable to Soviet subversion.

With Eisenhower's blessing, the Dulles brothers resurrected the dormant plot to topple Mossadegh and sent Kermit Roosevelt, a veteran CIA covert operator—whose grandfather Theodore had once sat in the White House—to Tehran in the spring of 1953 to make the necessary arrangements.

Roosevelt's plan, code-named "Operation Ajax," was really quite simple. In exchange for strong assurances of U.S. support, the Shah of Iran would issue a royal decree demanding that Mossadegh step down as prime minister and turn power over to General Zahedi, who would outlaw the Tudeh Party and negotiate a settlement in the ongoing oil dispute.

When the Shah announced the change of government on 16 August 1953, however, Mossadegh ignored him and responded instead by issuing a warrant for Zahedi's arrest. Not long afterward, Mohammed Reza Pahlavi flew to Rome for an unscheduled vacation, Zahedi went into hiding, and the CIA went back to the drawing board.

Forty-eight hours later, Kermit Roosevelt orchestrated what he later termed "a counter-coup" against Mossadegh. With help from Britain's MI6, Roosevelt distributed a quarter-million dollars in bribes to mobilize hundreds of pro-Shah mercenaries, who stormed into the streets chanting anti-government slogans and staged violent clashes with Mossadegh's supporters. Meanwhile, General Zahedi and right-wing military officers moved to restore order, rounding up Tudeh Party militants, arresting Prime

Minister Mossadegh, and inviting the Shah to return to Tehran in triumph.

Having convinced themselves that Iran was about to fall to communism, Eisenhower and the Dulles brothers had encouraged pro-American forces to overthrow a democratically elected Iranian leader and place an increasingly autocratic ruler back on the Peacock Throne.

"Throughout the crisis the United States government had done everything it possibly could to back up the Shah," Ike confirmed in his memoirs many years later. "Indeed, reports from observers on the spot in Teheran during the critical days sounded more like a dime novel than historical fact."

Partners: The Shah and the United States

From the American standpoint, Operation Ajax had a very happy ending. In June 1954, the Shah resolved the oil dispute amicably by establishing an international consortium that included AIOC and three U.S. petroleum giants, who would distribute the output from wells and refineries that were to remain under Iranian control.

A year later, he agreed to join the Central Treaty Organization, an anti-Soviet pact sponsored by the Eisenhower administration, and permitted the United States to establish electronic surveillance posts along Iran's border with Russia.

Then in 1957, the Shah established the SAVAK (a Farsi acronym for State Information and Security Organization), which, with help from the CIA, systematically silenced all opposition, imprisoning and torturing thousands of anti-Pahlavi activists.

The Shah sealed his partnership with the United States during the early 1960s, when Iran aligned itself with Israel under American auspices to curb Soviet influence among Arab nationalists like Egypt's Gamal Abdel Nasser.

Searching for Stability

America's Iran watchers worried, however, that the Shah's repressive domestic policies might backfire, sparking an anti-Western backlash against a regime that was spending too many of its petro-dollars on guns and too few on butter.

Just ten weeks after John F. Kennedy moved into the White House, riots erupted halfway around the world in Tehran. In May 1961, the new president established a National Security Council (NSC) task force to study the crisis in Iran.

Before the year was out, JFK's advisers concluded that the Iranian turmoil was home-grown, not communist-inspired, and feared that unless the Shah embraced economic modernization and political reform, his days were numbered. In April 1962, President Kennedy invited Mohammed Reza Pahlavi to Washington, where the two leaders reviewed a blueprint for stability in Iran.

Nine months later, the Shah unveiled his bold new "White Revolution," a set of "top-down" reforms designed to avert radical "bottom-up" change like Fidel Castro's "red revolution" in Cuba. Land reform, industrial growth, women's rights, and better schools were quite popular among Iran's emerging middle class, as were the U.S. Peace Corps volunteers who began arriving in the spring of 1963 to preach modernization.

Iranian landlords, on the other hand, felt threatened and resisted the White Revolution, as did clerics like Ruhollah Khomeini, a 61-year-old ayatollah who ridiculed the Shah as a U.S. puppet and denounced the American-backed reforms as "Westoxification." Most American officials, however, regarded Khomeini as little more than an annoying Islamic rabble-rouser and welcomed the Shah's decision in November 1964 to send him into exile, first to Turkey and then to Iraq.

By the late 1960s, Iran seemed to be a real success story for U.S. foreign policy at a time when Lyndon B. Johnson was increasingly preoccupied with the quagmire that he had inherited from JFK in Vietnam. Hundreds of U.S. corporations were investing in the Shah's economic miracle, thousands of Iranian students were flocking to the United States to attend college, and millions of barrels of oil were flowing from Iran to America's Cold War allies in Japan and Western Europe.

Convinced that the White Revolution was irreversible, Mohammed Reza Pahlavi vowed to make Iran a regional superpower and hosted a garish celebration in October 1971 to commemorate the 2500th anniversary of the founding of the Persian Empire by Cyrus the Great. Seven months later on his way home from a summit meeting with Soviet leaders in Moscow, President Richard Nixon, LBJ's successor, stopped in Tehran, where he made the Shah an offer he could not refuse.

As the war in Vietnam wound down, Nixon and NSC adviser Henry Kissinger explained, the United States was looking to scale back its military commitments in places like Southeast Asia and the Middle East. If Iran was willing to become America's partner and assume responsibility for ensuring political stability in the Persian Gulf, Nixon would permit the Shah to purchase any non-nuclear weapons system in the U.S. arsenal, including helicopter gunships, jet fighters, and guided-missile frigates.

The Shah embraced the new "Nixon Doctrine" enthusiastically. Indeed, between 1972 and 1977, he bought $13 billion worth of American military hardware and paid for it from the increased revenue generated by skyrocketing oil prices following the October 1973 Arab-Israeli War and the ensuing embargo imposed by the Organization of Petroleum Exporting Countries (OPEC).

The oil boom proved to be a mixed blessing for OPEC members like Iran, however, touching off an inflationary spiral that caused the cost of basic necessities to rise sharply and widened the gap between Iranian haves and have-nots.

When dissidents took to the streets to protest wasteful military spending, to appeal for better jobs, and to demand democratic reforms, the Shah unleashed a brutal crackdown and authorized the SAVAK and the Iranian army to use lethal force if necessary to quell the unrest. From his exile in Iraq, the Ayatollah Khomeini condemned the bloodshed and called for the overthrow of the American-backed tyrant.

The United States and the Iranian Revolution

President Jimmy Carter, who assumed office in January 1977, was highly skeptical of the Nixon Doctrine and deeply disturbed by the Shah's repressive policies, which ran counter to his own campaign promise to make human rights a central pillar of post-Vietnam U.S. foreign policy.

After Iranian exchange students chanted anti-Pahlavi slogans and clashed with local police outside the White House during the Shah's visit to Washington in late October, Carter took his guest aside and urged him privately to change course. Yet when Carter visited Tehran on New Year's Eve 1977, he felt obliged to offer a well publicized toast to Mohammed Reza Pahlavi, whose realm was "an island of stability in one of the more troubled areas of the world."

No American could make such a toast one year later.

On 8 January 1978, Iranian troops fired into a noisy pro-Khomeini crowd in the holy city of Qom, killing two dozen demonstrators and wounding more than 100 others. Much to the dismay of the Carter administration, the protests soon spread throughout Iran, bringing together an unlikely coalition of mullahs, merchants, and middle-class students who could only agree on one thing—that the Shah must go.

When heavily armed soldiers killed 400 protesters and injured 4,000 more in Tehran's Jaleh Square on 8 September, most observers expected him to go sooner rather than later. In early November, U.S. Ambassador William Sullivan drafted a cable informing Carter and his advisers that the time had come for "Thinking the Unthinkable"—an Iran without the Shah.

The end came quickly. After briefly exploring the possibility of a pro-American military regime, in which the Shah would have been reduced to little more than a figurehead, the Carter administration quietly encouraged the man who had ruled Iran for almost forty years to pack his bags.

On 16 January 1979, Shah Mohammed Reza Pahlavi boarded a Boeing 707 at Tehran's Mehrabad airport and headed off for exile in Egypt. Two weeks later, the Ayatollah Khomeini returned to Iran for the first time in fifteen years vowing to cleanse the country of all remaining influence of "the Great Satan," as he called the United States, and promising to establish an Islamic Republic.

Raised in a secular American society that was threatened by a secular Soviet menace, few U.S. policymakers expected Islam to play a significant role in Iranian politics, and fewer still understood Khomeini's brand of Shi'ism.

Uncertain about what the future held, U.S. diplomats worked with Prime Minister Mehdi Bazargan and other moderate leaders in Tehran to prevent a rupture in Iranian-American relations throughout the spring and into the summer. Meanwhile, Khomeini's youthful supporters organized themselves into battalions of "revolutionary guards" who harassed members of the old regime and denounced all things American.

On 23 October 1979, the White House confirmed that the Shah of Iran had checked into the Cornell University Medical Center in New York City for surgery on the lymphoma that would eventually kill him. Although Jimmy Carter insisted that this was a purely humanitarian gesture, it evoked bad memories of Operation Ajax a quarter-century earlier, when the CIA had conspired with the Shah to overthrow Mohammed Mossadegh.

Twelve days after Mohammed Reza Pahlavi arrived in Manhattan, Iranian students fiercely loyal to the Ayatollah Khomeini stormed the U.S. embassy in Tehran and captured 53 American diplomats, whom they would hold hostage for 444 days.

The hostage crisis poisoned Iran's relations with America, making Islam a dirty word and dominating the political discourse on Main Street and inside the Beltway.

Khomeini had not known about the embassy takeover in advance, but because this blow against "the Great Satan" was quite popular throughout Iran, he was able to use the crisis to build support for an Islamic Republic. Frustrated by the Ayatollah's unwillingness to negotiate, Carter approved a complex hostage rescue mission on 24 April 1980 that literally crashed and burned in the desert 300 miles southeast of Tehran, killing 8 American GI's and dooming the incumbent president's bid for reelection the following November.

A few minutes after President Ronald Reagan took the oath of office on 20 January 1981, Iran finally released the American hostages, but relations between the new administration in Washington and the Islamic Republic in Tehran remained frosty.

Antagonists: Iran and the United States since 1981

By the time that Reagan settled into the Oval Office, Khomeini's Iran was already locked in an increasingly bloody war with Saddam Hussein's secular Ba'athist regime in Iraq that would last eight years and claim half a million lives, two-thirds of them Iranian.

Clearly determined to stymie Iran's influence in the region, especially in Saudi Arabia and the Persian Gulf, and doubtless also eager to settle old scores, the Reagan administration tilted toward Iraq, providing Saddam Hussein with satellite reconnaissance of the battlefield, "dual-use" aircraft easily converted to military purposes, and $1.1 billion in agricultural credits.

For their part, the Iranians resorted to human wave assaults against Iraqi fortifications and channeled covert support to Islamic radicals like Lebanon's Hezbollah or "Party of God," whose operatives killed 241 U.S. Marines in a bombing at the Beirut Airport in 1983 and took seven American civilians hostage in the Lebanese capital during 1985.

A year later, President Reagan was humiliated after Hezbollah revealed that the White House had approved a half-baked "arms for hostages" deal with the Khomeini regime that came to be known as the Iran-Contra Affair.

The Iran-Iraq War ended in stalemate in August 1988, and many observers believed that Reagan's retirement to California the following January and Khomeini's death four months later would herald a new era in Iranian-American relations.

Saddam Hussein's invasion of Kuwait in August 1990 provided a painful reminder to Reagan's successor, George H. W. Bush, that "the enemy of my enemy is not always my friend." The United States was able to defeat Iraq in February 1991 without any help from Iran, whose efforts to export Islamic fundamentalism throughout the Middle East continued to make it a pariah in Washington.

Bush lost his bid for a second term a year and a half later less because of dissatisfaction with recent U.S. decisions in the Persian Gulf than because of the electorate's unhappiness with the state of the U.S. economy.

From the End of the Cold War to the Clash of Civilizations

More interested in fixing what was broken domestically than in rethinking American diplomacy, President Bill Clinton adopted a policy of "dual containment" that employed economic sanctions and military threats to prevent either Iraq or Iran from making trouble.

This approach resonated nicely with the notion, popularized by Harvard political scientist Samuel P. Huntington, that the post-Cold War world was witnessing "a clash of civilizations" between Islam and the West.

Clinton's rigid policies in the Persian Gulf, however, left America unprepared to make the most of remarkable developments in Tehran, where Iranian voters weary of two decades of political and religious turmoil elected Mohammed Khatami, an Islamic moderate, as president in May 1997.

Iran's new leader proceeded to stand Samuel Huntington on his head by calling for "a dialogue of civilizations."

Yet despite Khatami's eagerness to restore diplomatic ties with the United States severed during the earlier hostage crisis, and despite his denunciation of terrorism, the Clinton administration insisted that Iran must also halt its nuclear research program and cease its support for Islamic extremists in Lebanon and elsewhere.

A few hours after al-Qaeda brought down the World Trade Center on 11 September 2001, Mohammed Khatami sent condolences to Clinton's successor, George W. Bush, while thousands of young Iranians held a candlelight vigil in the streets of Tehran.

"Dubya" welcomed these goodwill gestures, but early in the new year he was outraged by an abortive Iranian attempt to run guns to Hamas, a Palestinian Islamist group that favored armed resistance against Israel. He was also disturbed to learn that Iran was moving ahead with plans to build a nuclear reactor capable of producing weapons-grade uranium at Bushehr.

Although Khatami reiterated his desire to improve relations, President Bush branded Iran a terrorist regime during his state of the union address on 29 January 2002 and made the Islamic Republic a charter member of "the Axis of Evil," along with Iraq and North Korea.

When the U.S. troops invaded Iraq fourteen months later to depose Saddam Hussein, it was Khatami's turn to condemn America. By late 2003 Iranian intelligence was working closely with Moktada al-Sadr and other Shi'a militants in Iraq, who were waging a guerrilla war against the American-controlled Coalition Provisional Authority in Baghdad.

In June 2005, Mahmoud Ahmadinejad, a founding member of Khomeini's revolutionary guards and a two-term mayor of Tehran, won an upset victory in the Iranian presidential elections. A hard-line Islamist who was critical of Mohammed Khatami's moderate domestic and foreign policies, Ahmadinejad called for a jihad against America and Israel, vowed to make Iran a nuclear power as soon as possible, and claimed that the Holocaust was a hoax perpetrated by an international Jewish conspiracy.

Although the United States had its hands full combating an ever-widening insurgency in Iraq, some of George W. Bush's top advisers, including Vice President Dick Cheney, privately welcomed the prospect of an Israeli preemptive strike against Iran's Bushehr nuclear complex and publicly hinted that regime change in Tehran should be next on America's "to do" list.

Cooler heads prevailed, but by the time that Bush left office in January 2009, American relations with Iran were colder than at any time since the hostage crisis thirty years earlier.

Obama and the Call for New Beginnings

During his 2008 presidential campaign, Barack Obama urged Americans to reexamine their attitudes toward Islam and indicated that if he were elected, he would consider meeting with anyone, including Mahmoud Ahmadinejad, in the interest of improving U.S. relations with the Muslim world.

While President Obama did not travel to Tehran, he delivered a stirring speech at Cairo University on 2 June 2009, in which he called for "a new beginning" in the troubled encounter between Americans and the peoples of the Middle East. Obama did not mention Mohammed Mossadegh by name, but he did acknowledge that "in the middle of the Cold War, the United States played a role in the overthrow of a democratically elected Iranian government."

He also pointed out that "since the Islamic Revolution, Iran has played a role in acts of hostage-taking and violence against U.S. troops and civilians." Despite all this bad blood, however, Obama insisted that the United States was now "prepared to move forward" toward a better relationship, if Iran was willing to reciprocate.

Thousands of Iranians watched Obama's speech over the Internet, and they heard this message loud and clear. President Ahmadinejad, on the other hand, dismissed the speech as mere rhetoric.

His opponents thought otherwise and hoped to derail his reelection campaign later that month. As election-day drew near, throngs of young people surged into Tehran's Jaleh Square to support Mir Hossein Mousavi, a charismatic Islamic reformer supported by Mohammed Khatami and other moderates.

Pro-government thugs took to the streets with knives and guns, however, savagely assaulting Mousavi's supporters, one of whom, 26-year-old Neda Agha Soltan, bled to death in an awful scene captured on a cell phone video that went viral on YouTube.

IRAN BEFORE AND AFTER THE SHAH: CLEARING A MISUNDERSTANDING

[…]

In many ways our situation is worse than the time of the Shah. The regime is much less tolerant, as the Shah didn't try to control people's private lives, and the laws were much better too, as they didn't include so much sexism and medieval punishments. The economy was better, and Iran wasn't the bad guy to most of the world, and Iranians could travel around the world without suspicion. In many ways the Shah tolerated his opposition better, although he allowed torture and censorship, they were used less relentlessly than now. So, no one can doubt that the regime which was in power was much better than this one.

However, I think it's a very narrow view of society to think everything is the regime and the laws. The Shah's modernization was focused on making Iran "look" modern, and yes, there was an artificial middle class which went to beaches with bikini and lived very similar to westerners, but I say "artificial" because they were really created by the Shah's economy and they were not representative of the majority of people, who became poorer and poorer and also felt indignant about the Shah's disregard for the clergy. So, they represented a false picture of Iranian society. They pretended that Iranians are a modern nation, while they weren't.

Our regime has regressed. Our society has progressed and rapidly.

That is why I ultimately think the Iranian society is in a better shape now that it was before. There are many dangers ahead of us that can undone everything — war, civil war, etc. But ultimately, I think Shah's progress was a fake one, while people's progress is real.

— "Iran Before and After the Shah: Clearing a Misunderstanding," by Kaveh Mousavi, Patheos, March 8, 2014

When the votes were counted in late June, Ahmadinejad was declared the winner, even though neutral observers detected unmistakable signs of wholesale electoral fraud. Barack Obama professed to be "deeply troubled" by events in Iran, but critics condemned him for not doing something more substantial.

Yet the painful truth was: What could he have done? Any form of U.S. intervention would quite likely have discredited Mousavi's "Green Revolution" in the eyes of many Iranians, who remembered the story of Operation Ajax all too well.

Moving Forward

Little has changed since June 2009. The American media continue to depict Mahmoud Ahmadinejad as a barbaric madman—Dr. Strangelove in a turban—while U.S. policymakers are beginning to worry that if the Stuxnet computer virus doesn't disable Iran's Bushehr nuclear reactor, the Israeli air force will.

Meanwhile, Iranians remain badly divided about the United States, with most men and women in the street favorably inclined toward the American people but deeply troubled by American policies toward the Muslim world, which Ahmadinejad continues to denounce as hypocritical and barbarous.

As they did throughout much of the twentieth century, the governments of America and Iran continue to view each other with fear and suspicion well into the second decade of the new millennium.

Yet reconciliation between these proud two nations is not impossible to imagine, even in an era dominated by the incendiary rhetoric of George W. Bush and Mahmoud Ahmadinejad.

One hundred years before Neda Agha Soltan was shot to death in Tehran and five years after Benjamin Labaree was murdered near Mount Ararat, Howard C. Baskerville, a Presbyterian missionary born in North Platte, Nebraska, died in faraway Tabriz on 20 April 1909 fighting alongside Iranian revolutionaries who eventually forced Shah Mohammed Ali Qajar to establish a constitutional monarchy.

Few Iranians and fewer Americans realize that at Constitution House in downtown Tabriz, there is a bust of Baskerville bearing the legend: "Patriot and Maker of History."

U.S.-Iran Relations Have Been Characterized by Missed Opportunities

Shaul Bakhash

Shaul Bakhash is the Clarence Robinson professor of history at George Mason University. The following viewpoint is based on his presentation at "U.S. Foreign Policy and the Modern Middle East," a Madeleine and W. W. Keen Butcher History Institute lecture sponsored by the American Institute for History Education and the Wachman Center for Civic and International Literacy of the Foreign Policy Research Institute, held June 25–27, 2009, in Philadelphia. In this essay, Bakhash, focuses a bit more on the economic interdependence of the United States and Iran and how the relationship might have turned out quite differently. According to Bakhash, relations have evolved from something like a patron-client relationship to a partnership to an adversarial relationship.

The U.S. has had relations with Iran ever since the last quarter of the nineteenth century. American missionaries have been in Iran even longer than that. But the United States' real engagement with Iran dates only from WWII. The relationship has generally been close, but it has been punctuated first by the involvement of the CIA in the coup of 1953 which overthrew a popular prime minister, Mohammed Mossadegh, and then by the Islamic Revolution of 1979, which led to a breach in relations that has not yet been repaired. Indeed, two countries that were

---

"The U.S. and Iran in Historical Perspective," by Shaul Bakhash, Foreign Policy Research Institute, September 28, 2009. Reprinted by Permission.

once close friends and allies now see each other, respectively, as the "Great Satan" and a member of an "Axis of Evil."

Looking at how some of the leading historians and analysts of the U.S.-Iranian relationship have dealt with this issue, it's interesting to note this constant sense of loss, of what might have been. Barry Rubin entitled his work on the relationship *Paved with Good Intentions*; James Bill subtitled his *Eagle and the Lion* with "The Tragedy of Iranian-American Relations." Gary Sick, a former member of the National Security Council, subtitles his "America's Tragic Encounter with Iran." A recent book by journalist Barbara Slavin plays on this idea of a relationship that might have been much better than it is, entitling her book *Bitter Friends, Bosom Enemies*.

Between 1945–79, the U.S.-Iranian relationship was in some ways similar to the U.S.-Saudi relationship, where the U.S. dealt with one ruling family. In the case of Iran, the U.S. dealt with one ruler, Mohammad Reza Shah Pahlavi, who came to the throne in 1941 and continued to rule for almost four decades. In this period, the relationship was governed by a number of enduring and persistent features.

First, on the American side, the interest in Iran was due in large part to the country's strategic location, bordering, on the one side, the Persian Gulf and on the other, at least until the collapse of the Soviet Union, sharing a very long border with America's previous adversary. Iran was also important because of its oil. During the Cold War, Iran was both a potential target of Soviet expansionism, against which it had to be protected, and a potential and often real ally in the struggle against the Soviet Union. Finally, as Iran grew wealthier from oil revenues, it became increasingly a market for U.S. goods, arms, industrial equipment, technology, investments, and, during the oil boom years after 1973, the employment of American technicians, advisers, specialists and the like.

On the Iranian side, first, the U.S. was seen as a potential protector, initially against the dominance of the two great powers that Iran had experienced throughout its 19th-century and early

20th-century history—Russia and Britain; and then against the Soviet Union. A second persistent feature of the U.S.-Iranian relationship was Iran's view of the U.S. not only as a patron and protector, but also as an ally in advancing what one scholar has called the Shah's dreams of grandeur; the idea that Iran could and should be a great power, at least in the region.

Iran's 19th–early 20th century history with Britain and Russia/ the Soviet Union included wars with both these powers. Iran lost territory to both, principally to Russia. Both countries were deeply involved in Iran's economy and trade, and both interfered extensively in Iran's internal affairs and politics. Beginning in the 19th century, Iran sought what I call a "third-country policy"—that is, trying to find a country that could counterbalance these two great powers. In the 19th century, it was sometimes Germany, sometimes France. In the 20th century, particularly beginning in WWII, Iran began to look to the U.S. But this older history of wariness of great powers has played a role in Iran's relations with the U.S. as well. A country that was seen for the most part of the period after 1941 as an ally, a great power in its own right, could also be seen as a country playing once again the imperialist role. As we have seen since the 1979 revolution, it is largely in this role that Tehran has viewed the U.S in the last three decades.

One can view the U.S.-Iranian relationship since WWII in four phases. First, from 1941–53, Iran sought a protector and friend; the Shah actively and determinedly sought to woo the U.S., to attract it into a closer relationship. Second, from 1953 to the late 1960s (post-overthrow of Mossadegh), with the restoration of the Shah, who had fled the country, to the throne, as the result of a coup engineered in large part by the CIA and British intelligence, was a period in which Iran was very dependent on the U.S.— on American protection, support, and aid. This was not quite a patron-client relationship, and Iran and the Shah's independence of the U.S. grew. But nevertheless, it was clear that the U.S. was the senior partner in the relationship. Third, in the period 1973–79, the relationship became much more of a partnership. The shah was much more stable at home, wealthier, and more adept at handling his foreign relations. He began to make demands. Fourth and finally, since 1979, the two countries have been adversaries and have had no direct political and diplomatic relations at all.

WWII and Post-WWII

When WWII broke out, Iran declared neutrality. But the Russians and British invaded Iran in August 1941 anyway. They did so principally for two reasons. First, Iran had had very close relations with Germany. The myth that the ruling monarch of the time was pro-fascist/German has now been addressed and dismissed. But there was a large German presence in Iran, and the British feared for the security of their oil wells in the south, and the Russians for their oil wells in Baku, across the Iranian border.

Secondly, once Hitler invaded Russia in spring 1941, the allies needed Iran's land route to supply the Russian army. This would not have been impossible under a neutral Iran, and therefore the Russians and British decided to invade Iran. They got rid of the shah and placed his son on the throne. This also brought American troops to Iran to facilitate the supplies that moved from the Persian Gulf across Iranian territory to the Soviet Union.

The Shah courted the U.S. assiduously in this period as protection against the two great powers that had occupied the country. On the whole, the U.S. was willing to be wooed and seduced. Early on they gave Iran considerable support. It was the U.S. that persuaded Russia and Britain to sign an agreement to withdraw their troops from Iran within six months of the end of hostilities in the war. The Russians' behavior in Iran was moderated because of the U.S. presence.

When at the end of WWII the Russians insisted on keeping their troops in Iran and supported a quasi-breakaway autonomous movement in the Iranian province of Azerbaijan, the U.S. was very helpful in pressuring the Russians to withdraw and end this support. Already during the war, a permanent feature of the U.S.-Iranian relationship had begun. The Americans sent advisors to assist in building up the Iranian army, police, and gendarmerie force and to assist in other areas of Iranian administration such as finance.

The shah, who was always ambitious to build up a large army, already began in this period what became a perennial theme in the relationship, which is to urge the Americans to supply his army with more advanced armaments.

Mossadegh and the Oil-Nationalization Crisis

This honeymoon period in the U.S.-Iranian relationship faced a crisis in 1951, during the movement to nationalize the Iranian oil industry. Iran's oil industry was the most important industry in the country. It was the principle source of foreign exchange revenues. It was the largest employer in the country. But it was British controlled. Iranians had no say in the management of the company, or production, or setting oil prices. For years, the British government had derived from the Iranian oil operation far more income than the Iranian government itself. In the late 1940s and then genuinely in 1951, there began a movement to nationalize the oil industry. This movement was led by Mossadegh, who became Prime Minister. The oil industry was in fact nationalized in March 1951. Then there began a two-year struggle between Iran and Britain over this act.

During the Truman administration, the U.S. government was supportive of Iran. The US was suspicious of the old imperial powers, and supported nationalist movements, which it thought were a good barrier to the spread of communism. There was genuine sympathy with the plight of the Iranians and their desire for more control of their oil industry. The Truman administration was often in the position of urging the British to be more forthcoming in meeting Iranian demands.

The British from the beginning were very unsympathetic to nationalization and decided that Mossadegh was not a reasonable man with whom they could deal. They sought to have him removed from office. They tried to persuade the U.S. to join them in a plot to overthrow him. Truman was not willing to go along with this idea, but as soon as the Eisenhower administration came in, it was very receptive. Both President Eisenhower's secretary of state, John Foster Dulles, and his brother Allen, the head of the CIA, were Cold Warriors. JFD believed that neutrality in the Cold War between the Soviet bloc and the U.S. was immoral. They joined the British in a plot which, after some wavering and uncertainty, did succeed in overthrowing Mossadegh in August 1953.

This was a seminal event in the modern history of Iran. The involvement of the CIA and British intelligence in a coup that overthrew a properly elected and very popular PM has remained seared into the Iranian historical imagination and has colored the relationship U.S.-Iranian relationship.

There were a number of other important repercussions of this U.S. involvement in the overthrow of Mossadegh. The Shah, who almost lost his throne over the affair, returned to Iran in August 1953 determined that this should never happen to him again. After 1953, there was increasing royal autocracy and intolerance for criticism, dissent, independent political parties, an independent press or an independent parliament.

Second, the shah's dependence on U.S. support was intensified and entrenched. In fact, having brought the shah back to power, the U.S. had a deep interest in seeing that his regime was stable and that he remained on the throne. Therefore, he was given not only moral and diplomatic support, but financial and other forms of aid as well.

In the minds of the Iranian political class, the impact of this U.S. involvement was two-fold. On the one hand, the idea that America was different from the older imperial powers persisted. The opposition, including Mossadegh's own party, the National Front, continued to believe that just as America had helped Iran against the imperialists in the past, it would come back to its senses and help them again.

On the other hand, the U.S., which had been seen as supportive of Iran's national interests, was now seen in another light. Both these trends of thinking persisted among the Iranian political class pretty much down to the time of the 1979 revolution, although the close alliance of the shah and the U.S. in these years, particularly in the late 1960s and 70s, these years of growing royal autocracy, clearly brought the Iranian belief in America's commitment to democracy, to put it mildly, under great strain.

These were also years in which the shah, both in terms of what he considered Iranian national interests and also because of his reliance on U.S. support, when Iran's foreign policy was very closely aligned with America's foreign policy. As a result, tensions with the USSR increased, and Iran was quick to join the Baghdad Pact, which saw Iran, Turkey, Pakistan and Britain allied together in a defense pact with the U.S. an informal partner.

This close U.S.-Iran alignment on foreign policy issues in the 1950s and the early 1960s was occurring at a time when elsewhere in the Middle East and Asia we saw the rise of nationalists governments. In the Middle East in particular, monarchies seemed to be falling like flies. Revolutionary officer regimes were coming to power in Egypt, Iraq and Syria. The great nations of Asia, India, China, and Indonesia, were leading a non-aligned movement. Therefore the shah, in terms of the broader trends in the Middle East and the region, seemed isolated. All this did not go very well with the younger generation in Iran, and broadly speaking, with the educated middle classes. The shah was pursuing a foreign policy, however sensible, one might argue, that went against the grain of the dominant political mood in the country.

The shah also developed, in this period, very close relations with Israel—not because of the U.S., but because of his own calculations of where Iran's interest lay. He saw all around him Arab regimes that were radical, increasingly allied to the Soviet Union, republics rather than monarchies. It made sense then, that the enemy of your enemy was your friend, and Iran's relations with Israel grew increasingly in this period. Not among all, but among a significant element in the population, it was unpopular.

The events surrounding what became known as the Status of Forces bill (1964)—the U.S. just signed a similar agreement with Iraq, SOFA—also proved controversial. These SOFA agreements the U.S. has with many countries where it stations troops are intended to protect American troops or military advisors in other countries from the "terrible" local courts. It in effect extends diplomatic immunity to military personnel serving in a foreign country. In 1964, the U.S. pressured a reluctant shah and a very reluctant parliament and reluctant government cabinet to sign a SOFA to cover American military personnel in Iran. The agreement immediately aroused memories of so-called capitulations which were very common in the region in the 19th century and which also exempted European nationals from the jurisdiction of native courts, Iranian courts in the case of Iran, Ottoman courts in the case of the Ottoman empire, Egyptian courts in the case of Egypt. In fact, Ayatollah Khomeini, who 15 years later was to lead an Islamic revolution in Iran, was expelled from the country for opposing very publicly the status of forces bill, which he called an agreement for the enslavement of Iran.

These were all ways in which the U.S.-Iranian relationship soured in the 1960s–70s. But the fact that the press, parliament, and political activity was controlled meant that the pros and cons of this close relationship the shah had reached with the U.S. were never openly discussed and public opinion was never openly articulated.

At the same time, the shah was never really a client of the U.S. In fact, he always chafed at having to do America's will and sought to escape this tutelage as quickly as he could. As his regime grew more stable, especially as Iran's oil revenues increased, he tried to shake the U.S. off. He did so increasingly successfully. The U.S. was preoccupied with Vietnam, the Nixon doctrine which led to the twin-pillars policy, the idea that regional powers allied with the U.S. should take responsibility for regional security, and that Iran and Saudi Arabia should shoulder more responsibility for Persian Gulf security, meant the U.S. relied more and more on the shah and more on him than on Saudi Arabia, which lacked Iran's size, population, or military clout. The Shah welcomed this, partly because it enhanced his own role and importance, and partly because he wanted to escape U.S. tutelage.

Then as oil prices exploded in 1973–74, Iran's oil revenues quadrupled overnight. The shah became not a debtor to the U.S. or the countries of Europe but a creditor. Iran not only gained enormous economic clout, but also offered the U.S. in a period of financial stringency and high oil prices a huge market for arms, industrial equipment, technology, and employment.

In this period the U.S. did make a number of serious errors in Iran, in addition to doing a number of things correctly. Aside from a brief period under President Kennedy's administration, when Kennedy pressured the shah to begin some reforms in Iran, particularly to break up the landed estates and give a greater share in land ownership to the peasantry, there was very little pressure in this entire period on the shah in the political sphere. The U.S. was pleased to see Iran stable and developing. It was developing spectacularly. The U.S. was pleased to have a large market for American goods. And as long as there was very little internal unrest, it seemed that everything was under control. The U.S. in this period, when it had weight and influence in Iran, missed opportunities to guide the shah politically, internally, in another direction.

Second, the U.S. was so pleased with the close alliance and with the apparent stability of the shah's regime that it began less and less to study closely the internal political situation. We know now that a time was reached when at the shah's insistence, the CIA agreed that it would not do its own intelligence work in Iran, but would rely on the shah's sources. When the boom in oil prices occurred and the shah decided to use this huge revenue, less wisely than other Gulf states, to try and catapult Iran into economic advancement and industrialization, the result was huge dislocations in the economy. Not only the U.S. but all the European countries were complicit in an economic policy that proved in the end very destabilizing to the shah's regime. The attempt to inject into the economy a significant amount of money in a very short period of time caused huge dislocations, and explains in part the discontent that helped fuel the 1979 Islamic revolution.

When that revolution took place, U.S.-Iranian diplomatic relations were broken and have not been restored since. The Islamic movement itself had from the beginning an anti-American component. Khomeini's revolution was against the shah, rooted primarily in internal problems. But it was also against the shah's close relations with the U.S. This stemmed from two very obvious factors. First, after all, the Americans had supported the shah, and the opposition therefore saw the U.S. as complicit in the shah's autocracy. One also cannot forget that Khomeini was exiled from his own country and spent 14 years initially in Iraq and then briefly in France as a result of opposing the SOFA.

Second, Khomeini both in leading the revolution and then in stabilizing it once the monarchy had been overthrown, played very adeptly on anti-American sentiment. The themes of anti-Americanism, of America as the shah's supporter, became themes not only of the revolutionary campaign but of post-revolutionary Iran as well.

Third, the seizure of the American embassy by student radicals and the taking of American diplomats as hostages had an enormous impact. Some 50 Americans remained hostages in Iran for 444 days, from November 1979 until the inauguration of President Reagan in 1981. This has left a deep impact on the American political imagination and also on the Iranian one. For the Americans, this was a searing experience; for the Iranians, it was a moment of triumph. The students who seized the embassy became overnight heroes.

Fourth, there was the U.S. position during the Iran-Iraq war. When the war broke out, the U.S. formally at least adopted a position of neutrality and did not supply arms to either side. America hoped the two sides would wear out and exhaust each other. But once Iran looked as if it might actually win the war and bring Saddam down, the U.S. began to support Saddam, not only diplomatically, but with intelligence. The U.S. also remained virtually silent when Saddam used chemical weapons against Iranian troops.

Finally, there has been the problem on the Iranian side of the U.S. attempt to sanction, isolate and demonize Iran and to view Iran as pursuing policies in Lebanon, on the Arab-Israeli conflict, and elsewhere, hostile to American interests.

It's not as if during these years there was no U.S. attempt to reach out to the Iranians or vice versa. The first president Bush, in his inaugural address, referring to U.S. hostages held in Lebanon by Iranian protégés, used the phrase "good will breeds good will." The Iranians did then help secure the release of these remaining U.S. hostages, but no good will came in reciprocation. Early in the Clinton administration, the president of Iran offered a U.S. company, Conoco, a large oil deal, but Clinton prevented the deal from going through. President Clinton himself, especially in his second term, attempted on a number of occasions to reach out to the Iranians without success.

So there were attempts in these years to repair relations. Why didn't they succeed? First, there was the legacy of the hostilities of the past on both sides. Second, there are concrete issues dividing the two countries. In any Iran-US rapprochement, Iran would want to see an end to U.S. sanctions against Iran, and an end to America's attempts to isolate Iran and deny it technology, trade, and credits. The U.S. would expect Iran to change its posture on Israel, to stop attempting to be a spoiler in the Palestinian-Israeli peace process, and to end its support for groups like Hezbollah in Lebanon and Hamas in the Gaza strip hostile to Israel. Also, for the U.S. there's the issue of Iran's nuclear program.

In addition, some forms of Iranian foreign policy behavior to which the U.S. particularly takes exception have become very entrenched. Iran's hostility to Israel has become a pillar of its foreign policy; its investment in Hezbollah in Lebanon is a long-standing policy. Iran and the U.S. are now competitors for influence in the Persian Gulf and the Middle East. Iran may be a small and weak country compared to the U.S., but it does have its visions of grandeur. It sees itself as the great power of the Persian Gulf region. It believes the U.S. must make space for it at the table in deciding the future of Iraq or Afghanistan. One can see how much at odds the Iranian position is from America's.

The events in Iran surrounding the June 23 elections will make it much more difficult for President Obama, who has tried to open a new page in U.S.-Iran relations, to allow his senior officials to sit at the table with Iran. But even had these events not taken place, U.S.-Iran relations would remain fraught with difficulties and obstacles.

America's Iranian Policies Are Driven by Energy Interests and International Security

Ken Pollack

In this viewpoint, Kenneth M. Pollack, a foreign policy expert on Iran and senior fellow at the Brookings Institution, gives a brief overview of U.S.-Iran relations over the last half century (up until the George W. Bush administration, during which time this piece was written). Notice that in Pollack's description of events, the interests and concerns of the citizens of the United States and Iran do not always line up with the interests and concerns of their respective governments. The United States' support for the repressive government of the shah helped fuel the rise of Iran's religious radicals who supported the Ayatollah Khomeini and contributed to worsening relations between the two nations.

Early U.S.-Iran Relations

In 1953, the United States played a significant role in a coup that removed democratically elected Premier Mohammed Mossadeq, restoring the Shah Mohammad Reza Pahlavi to power. Mossadeq sought to nationalize the oil industry whereas the Shah promoted a privatized system. Nationalization would allow Iran, rather than Great Britain, to profit from Iran's natural resource. As a result, the British urged the U.S. to aid the coup plot.

The British initially sought cooperation in planning the coup from President Truman, but he refused. After President Eisenhower's election in 1953, the British approached with the

"U.S.-Iran Relations," Robert Strauss Center for International Security and Law, University of Texas at Austin, August 2008. Reprinted by Permission.

coup idea. Eisenhower agreed and ordered the CIA to embark on Operation Ajax, a covert operation against Iran's government.

Operation Ajax undermined Mossadeq's government by bribing influential figures, planting false reports in newspapers and provoking street violence.[ii] On August 19, 1953, Mossadeq was forced from power and the Shah took over.

The U.S. benefited from this "˜shift' in political discourse; the U.S. gained control over Iranian oil and redistributed British production shares to U.S. companies. U.S. corporations acquired 40 percent of Iran's oil, Anglo-Iranian Oil's (the British corporation later renamed British Petroleum) share reduced to 40 percent, and French and Dutch companies acquired the other 20 percent.[iii]

The Iranians, on the other hand, did not benefit from the change in government nor did they reap the profits of its natural resource, oil.

The Revolution

The U.S.-supported coup (1953) ushered in two decades of dictatorship under the Shah, who relied heavily on U.S. aid and arms. During this period, Iran's society changed and modernized too rapidly for some opponents of the regime.

President Carter criticized the Shah's regime and its poor human rights record. The Shah, understanding that he depended on U.S. support, responded to Carter's request for change by taking steps towards liberalization. Carter, in turn, better appreciated the strategic importance of Iran both in the Middle East and for the United States in general: the U.S.-Iran alliance helped balance Soviet influence in the region.

The Iranian people, on the other hand, grew weary of repression and corruption, which the Iranians believed was inextricably linked to the United States. Some Iranians wanted a sense of stability and order and called for the traditions of Islam. Many Iranians looked to Ayatollah Khomeini for guidance and leadership in their opposition against the Shah. Khomeini regarded the Shah's regime as corrupt and illegitimate and referred to the U.S. as the "Great

Satan." At the request of the Iranian prime minister, the Shah left Iran on January 16, 1979. On February 1, 1979, Khomeini became the new leader of Iran.

Iranian Hostage Crisis

On November 4, 1979, a group of Iranian students stormed the American Embassy in Tehran and took 63 American Embassy personnel hostage. The specific grievance of the students (the hostage takers) focused on the Shah and his relationship with the U.S. In October 1979, U.S. officials learned the Shah was diagnosed with cancer. The Shah requested entry to the U.S. for medical treatment; President Carter rejected his request. After a vigorous campaign led by influential U.S. Shah supporters, the Shah was admitted into the United States.

The arrival of the Shah to the U.S. instigated Iranian unrest, which led to the invasion of the U.S. Embassy. It evoked memories of the 1953 coup and aroused fear that the U.S. was planning another coup to restore the Shah to power.[iv] In short, for the students who took over the Embassy, for the Iranian revolutionary officials who supported them, and for much of Iran, the taking of the Embassy was a response to the 1953 coup against Mossadeq.[v]

The U.S. responded to the situation through economic and diplomatic pressures. President Carter stopped U.S. oil imports from Iran, froze all Iranian assets in U.S. banks, and, with the exception of humanitarian goods, the U.S. ceased all trade with Iran. However, the economic sanctions and diplomatic pressures did not compel a hostage release. The U.S. then responded with a failed military action, resulting in the deaths of eight Americans. The hostage crisis served as the defining moment of the U.S.-Iran relationship for Americans.

Beyond the Hostage Crisis

Within a day of Reagan taking the oath of presidency, the hostages were released and returned stateside. However, during President

Reagan's administration, there was little to no improvement in U.S.-Iran relations. In 1983, Hezbollah conducted a series of anti-American terrorist attacks, and in 2003, the U.S. Supreme Court decided that Iran supported the terrorist organization. The Iran-Contra scandal followed the Hezbollah attacks. During the Iran-Contra scandal, the U.S. illegally sold weapons to Iran and used the profits to support the Contras in Nicaragua.

Despite the series of events with Iran in the 1980s, it was the accidental shooting down of a commercial airline by the U.S. that increased the hostilities between the U.S. and Iran. In 1988, the USS *Vincennes* shot down an Iranian commercial flight in Iranian air space over the Strait of Hormuz—290 Iranians died. Although the U.S. paid a compensation of $61.8 million to Iran, the U.S. never paid for the lost aircraft nor did they offer an official apology to Iran.

Thawing Relations?

The election of reformist Mohammad Khatami in 1997 brought a sense of optimism for U.S.-Iran relations. Throughout his campaign and post-election, Khatami expressed that he wanted to improve Iranian relations with the U.S. In his first major campaign speech, Khatami suggested that if the U.S. changed its bad behavior, the U.S. and Iran could have normal relations.[vi] This was a major shift from the past leadership of Khomeini who believed that Iran and the U.S. could never have normal relations.

Although the Clinton Administration welcomed Khatami's election, they remained vigilant and cautious of the sincerity of Khatami's rhetoric toward the U.S. Although Khatami indicated that the time was not yet right for direct bilateral discussions, he argued that the two countries begin to build relations through more informal, cultural exchanges.[vii]

Not too long after Khatami made these statements, the Clinton administration sent an American wrestling team to compete in Iran. The U.S. and Iran soon followed by allowing more open travel between the two countries to further encourage and facilitate people-to-people exchanges.[viii] The U.S. even lifted the embargo on two import items: rugs and pistachios.

However, the amicable exchanges ultimately stalled. Iran's conservatives remained unwilling to make further concessions and the U.S. was equally unwilling to negotiate terms of discussions including changes in Iranian policy on Israel, nuclear energy, and support for terrorism.

Axis of Evil

There have been no improvements in U.S.-Iran relations during the Bush Administration. In his State of the Union Address in 2002, President Bush labeled Iran as part of the 'Axis of Evil,' outraging the Iranian leadership. Iran responded with a public statement: "the Islamic Republic is proud to be a target of the hate and anger of the world's greatest evil; we never seek to be praised by American officials."[ix]

However, in 2003, Iran did offer a proposal trying to ease strained relations between the two rivals. Iran put several different issues on the table including an offer, within the framework of the negotiations, to disarm Hezbollah and turn it into a mere political organization. Secondly, the offer included an end of all support for Islamic jihad and Hamas, and provisions that Iran would encourage the Palestinians to go a political route, rather than military route, in their dealings with Israel.[x] The U.S. rejected the offer. Overall, the rhetoric of the Bush administration has been that Iran is a threat to not only the United States, but also to the international community.

Implications of U.S.-Iran Relations

U.S.-Iran relations are inextricably linked to the energy interests and security of the international community. Over 20 percent of **world oil supply** is transported daily through the Strait. If already tense relations were to escalate between the U.S. and Iran, Iran could retaliate by attempting to close or disrupt traffic in the **Strait of Hormuz**. This, in turn, may result in an armed confrontation between the U.S. and Iran, which would undoubtedly involve the Middle East region as a whole.

Endnotes

[i] The Brookings Institution, Interview with Kenneth M. Pollack (January 24, 2005). Online. Available: http://www.brookings.edu/interviews/2005/0124iran_pollack.aspx. Accessed: December 4, 2007.

[ii] Dan De Luce, "The Spectre of Operation Ajax," The Guardian (August 20, 2003). Online. Available at: http://www.guardian.co.uk/comment/story/0,3604,1021997,00.html. Accessed: December 4, 2007.

[iii] Larry Everest, "The U.S. & Iran: A History of Imperialist Domination, Intrigue and Intervention" Revolution, no. 90 (May 27, 2007). Online. Available at: http://rwor .org/a/090/iran-pt2-en.html. Accessed: December 4, 2007.

[iv] Kenneth M. Pollack, The Persian Puzzle: The Conflict Between Iran and America (New York: Random House, 2004), p 155.

[v] Kenneth M. Pollack, The Persian Puzzle: The Conflict Between Iran and America (New York: Random House, 2004), p 155.

[vi] Kenneth M. Pollack, The Persian Puzzle: The Conflict Between Iran and America (New York: Random House, 2004), p 310.

[vii] Kenneth M. Pollack, The Persian Puzzle: The Conflict Between Iran and America (New York: Random House, 2004), p 315.

[viii] Kenneth M. Pollack, The Persian Puzzle: The Conflict Between Iran and America (New York: Random House, 2004), p 321.

[ix] Kenneth M. Pollack, The Persian Puzzle: The Conflict Between Iran and America (New York: Random House, 2004), p 352.

[x] DemocracyNow.org, The Secret Dealings of Israel, Iran, and the United States. Online. Available: http://www.democracynow.org/2007/9/25/the_secret_dealings_of_israel_iran. Accessed: December 4, 2007.

Iran Is a Land of Social, Political, and Economic Contradictions

Karim Sadjadpour

In this viewpoint, Karim Sadjadpour, expert on Iran and policy analyst at the Carnegie Endowment for International Peace, answers some questions about Iranian society and how it has changed over the years. He points out how those changes have been influenced by—and in turn have influenced—Iran's political climate, economy, international relations, and how the country is viewed by other nations. Sadjadpour points out that Iran is a society with many cultural contradictions, and economic ones as well—despite having a great deal of oil wealth, Iran's economy still struggles.

Q&A with Karim Sadjadpour, an associate at the Carnegie Endowment for International Peace and the author of "Reading Khamenei: The Worldview of Iran's Most Powerful Leader."

How has Iranian society changed over the 33 years since the revolution?

Demographically, Iran is a much different society than it was 33 years ago. Its population has grown from around 35 million in 1979 to approximately 75 million today. Before the revolution Iranians were a predominantly rural people (around 55 percent), while three decades later a large majority of Iranians (more than 70 percent) are urban dwellers.

"Iran Then and 33 Years After the Revolution," by Karim Sadjadpour, WGBH Educational Foundation, February 1, 2012. Reprinted by Permission.

Visitors to Iran are often struck by the society's many dichotomies: Female education and literacy rates have increased dramatically since 1979, but women's rights have been curtailed.

The median age of Iranian society is 27, but the median age of the country's powerful political players—including the Supreme Leader, Guardian Council and Assembly of Experts—is well over 70.

Before the revolution, a secular autocracy presided over a largely traditional population, while today a religious autocracy rules over an increasingly secularized polity. (According to one oft-told joke, "Before the revolution people used to drink outside their homes and pray inside their homes; after the revolution people pray outside and drink inside.")

Thirty-three years ago Iranian society was steeped in revolutionary fervor. Today it suffers from revolutionary fatigue. This is one reason, among many, why Iran's 2009 uprising did not have the same durability as the popular uprisings which have unsettled and unseated numerous Arab dictatorships. People may aspire for revolutionary ends, but there's no romanticism about, and limited appetite for, revolutionary means.

How has the political climate changed?

The story of the Iranian revolution and its aftermath was perhaps most incisively articulated by reformist thinker Mostafa Tajzadeh, who's currently in prison. Before the revolution, Tajzadeh said, Iranians enjoyed all types of freedoms save for political freedom, which the revolution was meant to rectify. After the revolution, Iranians not only failed to attain political freedom, but they lost other freedoms in the process.

In some ways the political climate in Iran has come full circle over the last 33 years. In the first decade of the revolution there was a cult of personality around the revolution's father, Ayatollah Khomeini, whose word was considered sacrosanct.

After Khomeini's death in 1989, there was a two-decade struggle between pragmatic forces that believed the Islamic Republic needed to evolve with the times, and revolutionary purists, led by Supreme Leader Ayatollah Ali Khamenei, who believed that compromising on revolutionary ideals could unravel the entire system, just as perestroika did the Soviet Union.

Khamenei patiently but decisively prevailed, and in recent years his followers have attempted to create for him a similar cult of personality. Given his inferior clerical credentials, however, he has sought legitimacy in the military barracks more than the mosques.

Indeed perhaps the biggest difference over the past three decades has been the rise of the Revolutionary Guards as a political and economic force. The Islamic Republic is increasingly a military autocracy cloaked in clerical garb.

What is Iran's standing in the international community today?

Iran's international standing has also come full circle. The combination of the revolution, the hostage-taking of U.S. diplomats, and the eight-year war with Iraq turned Iran into an isolated pariah state for much of the 1980s.

After Khomeini's death and the end of the war, under Presidents Rafsanjani and then Khatami, Iran made it a priority to reconstruct its war-torn economy and repair its foreign relations.

Over the last several years, a multitude of factors— Ahmadinejad's bellicosity, the regime's brutal suppression of peaceful protesters, and the Obama administration's unprecedented but unreciprocated attempts at engagement—have in many ways returned Iran to relative isolation. To make matters worse, its only consistent ally since 1979, the Assad regime in Syria, is on the verge of collapse.

In a recent BBC survey of 27 countries, including non-Western countries such as China, Nigeria, and the Philippines, Iran was "the most negatively viewed of all countries rated," including North Korea. Iran had only a 16 percent favorability rating.

This is a sore point for many Iranians, who are fiercely proud, nationalistic and aspire to play an important role on the global stage.

What is the state of Iran's economy compared with 33 years ago?

The Iranian economy remains heavily oil-dependent, but decreased domestic production (due to an aging oil infrastructure, sanctions, and limited foreign investment) and increased domestic energy consumption (due to a population boom) have meant that Iran's oil exports have gone from 5m barrels in 1978 to a bit more than 2m barrels per day in 2012.

Given growing energy demand from countries like China and India, coupled with political risk in the Middle East, the Iranian economy has benefited from an unprecedented oil windfall.

According to some estimates, of the approximately $1 trillion in total oil income Iran has earned over the last century, a remarkable 60 percent was earned since the election of President Mahmoud Ahmadinejad in 2005.

Despite this natural wealth, the economy remains the Islamic Republic's Achilles heel, and people complain incessantly about the country's rampant inflation and unemployment, as well as endemic mismanagement and corruption.

Putting aside economic facts and figures, on an anecdotal level the sense of economic dismay among many Iranians has been heightened in recent years when visiting their thriving neighbors Turkey and Dubai, whom they have historically viewed with a degree of cultural superiority.

What is the state of Iranian ideology today?

I would argue that there are three remaining symbolic pillars of Iran's revolutionary ideology: "Death to America," "Death to Israel," and the veil, or hejab, which symbolizes Islamic piety.

These three pillars have in a way metastasized. They've become an inextricable part of the regime's identity and are likely to remain so as long as Ayatollah Khamenei remains Supreme Leader.

On a societal level, however, the utopian revolutionary ideology of 1979 has produced widespread disillusionment three decades later. Many analysts in Tehran liken it to the last decade of the

Soviet Union, when few true believers remained, even among regime insiders.

In contrast to Mikhail Gorbachev, however, Iran's leadership apparently is still prepared to use widespread and sustained repression rather than relinquish power.

As the late George Kennan once wrote about the Soviet Union, Iran's lack of ideological legitimacy has necessitated coercive legitimacy:

> *"Let it be stressed again that subjectively these men probably did not seek absolutism for its own sake. They doubtless believed—and found it easy to believe—that they alone knew what was good for society and that they would accomplish that good once their power was secure and unchallengeable. But in seeking that security of their own rule they were prepared to recognize no restrictions, either of God or man, on the character of their methods. And until such time as that security might be achieved, they placed far down on their scale of operational priorities the comforts and happiness of the peoples entrusted to their care."*

In terms of how Iranian ideology resonates abroad, the young Iranian scholar Mohammad Tabaar put it best when he said, "There was a time when Iran would rely on its revolutionary ideology to project power. Today, Iran uses its power to project ideology." In other words, as witnessed over the last year in the Arab world, Iran has increasingly few constituents in the Arab and Muslim world who wish to import their ideology. Instead Tehran has had to struggle to export it, increasingly via force and intimidation.

The Consequences of the 1979 Hostage Crisis Still Echo

Nick Amies

This viewpoint (which was first published in 2009), focuses on one particular event in the history of U.S.-Iran relations—what was known in the United States as the hostage crisis. It occurred in 1979, when Iranian Islamist students took over the US Embassy in Tehran and held fifty-two Americans hostage for 444 days. Here, Nick Amies, an international journalist specializing in geopolitical and geostrategic issues, details the event and reports on how the situation influenced subsequent diplomacy and attitudes in both the United States and Iran—and how, as of the first year of the Obama administration, it still informs policy and opinion in both nations.

Thirty years on from the capture of the US embassy in Tehran by Islamist students, the consequences of that event still reverberate through Iran and its relations with the United States.

The latent unease and unrest in Iran was once again visible Wednesday on the Islamic Republic's Day of National Confrontation against World Imperialism—the anniversary of the 1979 seizure of the US embassy in Tehran by Islamist students in support of the Iranian Revolution.

Thousands of supporters of Iranian President Mahmoud Ahmadinejad marked the 30th anniversary of the takeover of the US compound by filling the streets around the closed embassy in a state-organized anti-US rally chanting slogans such as "Death to America" and "Death to Israel."

"Consequences of 1979 hostage crisis still influencing US-Iran relations," by Nick Amies, Deutsche Welle, April 11, 2009. Reprinted by Permission.

Nearby, security forces clashed with opposition supporters and anti-Ahmadinejad protestors, still smarting from the disputed reelection of the president in June. The demonstrators, many of whom wore the green colors of failed presidential candidate Mir-Hossein Mousavi, shouted "Death to the dictator" as police responded with tear gas.

Both sides seemed to be capitalizing on the anniversary of the capture of the US embassy 30 years ago to renew confrontations which may have been suppressed since the weeks of unrest following the presidential elections but have not been eradicated.

Significant anniversary for both sides of Iranian political divide

The Nov. 4 date holds significance for both sides. Supporters of the regime see the capture of the US embassy as a pivotal event in the rise of the Islamic Republic and an unprecedented success against the United States. It remains a source of pride which fuels the belief that a sovereign Iran can be strong and independent in the face of US hegemony.

"We continue to hear very hostile rhetoric harking back to the period of the hostage crisis from Iran's leaders," Anthony Dworkin, a senior policy fellow and expert on US foreign policy at the European Council on Foreign Relations, told Deutsche Welle. "Ahmadinejad continues to very much play that card. The view from outside Iran is that Ahmadinejad and his support relies on this feeling of intense antagonism between Iran and the United States. People see a vested interest in stoking up these feelings on Ahmadinejad's part."

For opposition supporters, the anniversary marks the moment when the door to diplomacy and engagement in the world was slammed shut; a door that moderate Iranians hope to force open for the good of the nation, allowing Iran to fully rejoin the international community.

"There is a feeling in Iran that other regimes would have been more open to engagement and less invested in a stance of hostility towards the west," Dworkin added. "The moderates would undoubtedly have been more open to negotiations with the US."

This view was supported recently by Iran's top dissident cleric Grand Ayatollah Hossein Ali Montazeri who said that the capture of the US embassy and the holding of US citizens as hostages was a mistake.

"The occupation of the American embassy at the start had the support of Iranian revolutionaries and the late Imam Khomeini and I supported it too," he said. "But considering the negative repercussions and the high sensitivity which was created among the American people and which still exists, it was not the right thing to do. Principally an embassy is part of that country and occupying an embassy of a country which was not at war with us was like declaring a war against that country. It was not a correct thing."

Hostage crisis continues to color US perception of Iran

Certainly the repercussions from the 1979 US hostage crisis rumble on in the current relations between the United States and Iran, adding weight to the belief of moderates like Montazeri that the event was highly detrimental to Iran's standing not only with the United States but in the wider western world.

"The embassy and hostage crisis on 1979 lay at the roots of the pretty widespread feeling in the United States that Iran is a hostile and threatening country and that dates back to the time of the Islamic Revolution," Dworkin said. "It still affects they way people in the US feel about Iran, even though more recently the whole nuclear issue has colored that, but I think the events around the whole hostage crisis are still resonant in the US because relations have been pretty frozen since then and there hasn't really been a chance to set a new tone."

Despite the continuing anti-US rhetoric and the freeze in relations, there have been moves by US President Barack Obama to reach out to Iran through his engagement strategy, a very

Thirty-Six Years After the Revolution, Where Is Iran Now?

[...]

Iran has made commendable strides in many areas since the 1979 Islamic Revolution. From 1980 to 2012, Iran's Human Development Index (HDI) value—which takes into account lifespan, access to education and standard of living—increased by 67%, a rate of growth that was twice the global average. As of 2012, Iran's HDI value sat at 0.742, which put the country into the "high human development category." Access to electricity and piped water in rural areas, life expectancy, infant mortality and access to health care have all markedly improved. The literacy rate, which stood at 36% in 1976 and at just 25% for females, stands at 99% for males and females ages 15–24. Tertiary education has also never been so widely attainable by the Iranian population, with more than 2 million Iranian students enrolled at a university, over 60% of whom are women.

[...]

To be sure, Iran has a long way to go on its road to developing a better society for all Iranians. The human rights situation undoubtedly has room for ample improvements. The country is also beset by corruption, with the vice president in the Hassan Rouhani administration even saying the corruption "of the century" occurred during the Mahmoud Ahmadinejad era. High levels of inflation, unemployment and a bloated bureaucracy have also contributed to a "brain drain," or the emigration of many educated Iranians.

Iran's political arena is also a scene of fierce and counterproductive factional infighting, with almost all former heads of past administrations having been accused or humiliated, and having their credibility put into question by rivals. This domestic political struggle has swallowed some of the most prominent disciples of the revolution.

However, with all of its shortcomings, the Islamic Republic of Iran remains a political reality. It has firmly entrenched roots in Iran and now garners substantial geopolitical clout throughout the Middle East. After 36 years of overcoming what many thought were insurmountable obstacles, Iran has remained a strong and stable state. This is both testimony to impressive statecraft and

> demonstrates the necessity of a detente among the countries in the region, the West and this power that is here to stay.
>
> — "36 years after the revolution, where is Iran now?" by Seyed Hossein Mousavian, Al-Monitor, February 10, 2015.

different foreign agenda to the previous Bush administration's policy of confrontation.

While there have been some counter offers from Iran, they fall short of the clear-cut statements that the US is looking for. The experts believe this has much to do with the complexity of the situation within Iran.

Obama's engagement strategy causing unease in Tehran

"It's clear that the US wants to reopen dialogue and we've seen a lot from Obama; his praise of the Iranian people, his shift in language, his constant stressing of the legitimate interests of Iran and its dignity, civilization and so on," said Dworkin. "On the other hand, the political situation in Iran is going to make it difficult for the regime to respond positively to that. Domestically, it would be very hard for Ahmadinejad to go too far too quickly in responding to the US."

"Obama too is under pressure to show that the engagement strategy is yielding results. I think there are strong reasons on both sides to pursue an engagement strategy but the political context makes it quite difficult for both countries to spin this out for too much longer."

Dr. Josef Braml from the German Council on Foreign Relations believes that Obama's engagement policy could make life more uncomfortable for Iran's current regime and have a detrimental effect on a possible thawing of relations.

"Obama offered an open hand, he unclenched his fist but the Iranian leadership has bitten it," Braml told Deutsche Welle. "For Iran, this approach has caused problems because if someone approaches you with a smiling face, he shows the rest of the world that he's open. If you're not willing to accept that then it will be easier for Obama to get other countries on board which may have been reluctant to take a stand against Iran. Being open and cooperative and not being rewarded for that is an argument for stronger sanctions."

"But I think there is still a chance of restoring ties by engaging Iran and involving Iran as part of the solution rather than part of the problem," Braml added. "This would give the Iranian leadership some acknowledgment. There is no longer any talk about regime change and more talk about how the Iranians can be part of international solutions."

VIEWPOINTS ON
MODERN WORLD HISTORY

CHAPTER 2

US-Iran Relations Today

Preface

The Joint Comprehensive Plan of Action (JCPOA)—also known as the Iran nuclear deal—was thought by many to be a great solution to a vexing problem, but the solution itself was complex and not without controversy. The basics of the deal were that Iran would give up its nuclear weapons program (for the term of the agreement), and in turn the United States (and other signatories to the deal) would remove economic sanctions against Iran. Many Americans hailed the deal as a necessary step toward preventing nuclear war in the Middle East. In addition, its supporters believe that by removing sanctions and opening Iran to the rest of the world, Iran will quickly remodernize and, as the economy improves and the citizens have more interactions with the West, the radical leaders of the country would have less influence—and thereby Iran would be less of a danger in ways that go beyond nuclear bombs and include support of terrorism in other nations.

However, many people are convinced that the risks to US security, and particularly the security of Israel, are not worth the potential benefits of the deal. After the 2016 US presidential election, more of those people are in positions of power in Washington.

In this chapter, you will hear from commentators who argue that this resistance is due to a fundamental misunderstanding of the motivations and goals of Iran, commentators who think the danger from Iran has always been overblown, and from some who think the problems between the two nations aren't going to be solved by the JCPOA and that the agreement only escalates the problem.

You will also read viewpoints that analyze how far away Iran is from getting a nuclear bomb, how that may be further than many politicians are suggesting, and why some world leaders are interested in overestimating that time line.

The Iran Deal Won't Make Us Safer

John Simpson

John Simpson, world affairs editor of BBC News, does not agree that the Iran nuclear deal will make the world a safer place. But his disagreement is based on reasons that are different from what you might expect. In this viewpoint, Simpson explains how a mostly pro-Western, moderate majority in Iran struggles with conservative revolutionaries, which make up a minority of the population yet exercise a great deal of power over elected officials. The Iran deal will be beneficial for the moderate majority, though not to the conservative minority. The threat from Iran was exaggerated by Israel and the American right, Simpson says, but the threat from Saudi Arabia could well increase as a result of the deal.

A fter the Vienna agreement over Iran's nuclear programme was announced, Valiasr Avenue, the long, snaking road that brings traffic southwards and downhill from the middle-class suburbs of northern Tehran to the city centre, was blocked until 2am. Excited, relieved and optimistic, people piled into their cars and headed out to celebrate, hooting their horns, singing and chanting. For Barack Obama and the western leaders, the agreement seems to offer a new start after 36 confrontational years. But for millions of middle-class people in northern Tehran, it promises something even more enticing: the chance to weaken the control that the religious conservatives have maintained over everyday life since 1979.

"John Simpson: The Iran deal won't make the world much safer," by John Simpson, New Statesman Media Group, July 16, 2015. Reprinted by Permission.

It has been hard, over the years, to explain to western readers and viewers the deep contradictions of Iran, one of the world's least-reported-on major countries. The problem is that we think we know what the Islamic Republic is all about. We see the pictures of black-robed demonstrators in the streets denouncing the west and all its works. We recall the former president Mahmoud Ahmadinejad, with his unshaven face and simian eyes, and think that he speaks for an entire nation of extremists. We assume, therefore, that Iran's nuclear programme is intended to wipe out Israel and threaten western interests. And, as a result, we get Iran wrong every time.

The reality is that it is a highly complex political society—too complex for its own good—in which, for nearly 40 years, the old conservative revolutionaries have battled against the instinctively pro-western, relatively liberal instincts of a clear majority of its people. Even now, the conservatives manage to keep a grip on society through the structure of the state, which gives the unelected religious leader more authority than the elected president, and through the system of religious policing, which forces everyone to toe the line.

Every time the liberal section of society gets the chance to celebrate a victory over the conservatives, it does so in style—hence the parade of honking vehicles up and down Valiasr Avenue on 14 July. For the people leaning out of the windows and waving pictures of their foreign minister, Mohammad Javad Zarif, who led the negotiations to their successful conclusion, the agreement signals an end to sanctions and confrontation with the west. No wonder Iran's conservatives are nervous about the deal. It probably ensures that the markedly liberal president, Hassan Rowhani, will be re-elected in 2017; and it will make Iranian society more "westoxicated" (an old revolutionary term) and even harder to control.

Will it prevent Iran from having nuclear weapons? The agreement doesn't, on the face of it, seem particularly watertight, so Iran will likely be able to get around it if it wants. Yet there has never been any serious indication that Iran—even the Iran of the

Iran Deal Makes World a Safer Place, Says US President

One year on from implementation of the Joint Comprehensive Plan of Action (JCPOA), the US president said the agreement with Iran "must be measured against the alternatives." Meanwhile, Behrouz Kamalvandi, deputy head of the Atomic Energy Organization of Iran (AEOI) for International, Legal and Parliamentary Affairs, is on a two-day visit to Moscow to discuss progress with the JCPOA.

A statement from the US president's office yesterday said the deal had achieved "significant, concrete results in making the United States and the world a safer place", adding, "this historic understanding … has rolled back the Iranian nuclear program and verifiably prevents Iran from obtaining a nuclear weapon."

According to Iran's *MEHR* news agency, Kamalvandi was invited to Moscow by Nikolay Spassky, deputy director general for international affairs at Russian state nuclear corporation Rosatom, "to discuss bilateral and technical issues."

Signed in July 2015 by Iran and the E3/EU+3 (China, France, Germany, Russia, the UK and the USA—also referred to as the P5+1—plus the European Union), the JCPOA officially began on 16 January last year. Under its terms, Iran agreed to limit its uranium enrichment activities, eliminate its stockpile of medium-enriched uranium and limit its stockpile of low enriched uranium over the next 15 years. Implementation Day followed IAEA verification that Iran had fulfilled key commitments spelled out under the JCPOA.

[…]

The US president's statement, which did not give Barack Obama's name, said Iran's nuclear program "faces strict limitations and is subject to the most intrusive inspection and verification program ever negotiated to monitor a nuclear program." Iran has reduced its uranium stockpile by 98% and removed two-thirds of its centrifuges, the statement added.

"Iran has not enriched any uranium at the Fordow facility, nor used advanced centrifuges to enrich … In short, Iran is upholding its commitments, demonstrating the success of diplomacy … There is no question, the challenges we face with Iran would be much worse if Iran were also on the threshold of building a nuclear weapon," it said.

The president stressed that the JCPOA was the result of "years of work" and represents an agreement between the world's major powers. The agreement "must be measured against the alternatives—a diplomatic resolution that prevents Iran from obtaining a nuclear weapon is far preferable to an unconstrained Iranian nuclear program or another war in the Middle East," it concluded.

[…]

— "Iran deal makes world a safer place, says US president," World Nuclear Association, January 17, 2017.

conservatives—wants nuclear weapons. What it seeks is the status that generating energy by nuclear means seems to confer; for the most part (and aside from the terrorist attacks it has carried out), Iran has been relatively timid in international affairs.

It is a country with great imperial pretensions and it feels that British and American machinations have historically prevented it from exercising real power in the region. What power it has is exercised through the Shia nexus, linking it with Hezbollah in Lebanon, the Assad government in Syria, the Shia parties in Iraq and Shia groups in the Gulf. Iran is not and cannot be an existential threat to Israel but it can be a major diplomatic and military nuisance—hence the bitter condemnation of the Vienna deal by Binyamin Netanyahu.

Hence, too, the fears of Saudi Arabia and the Gulf rulers. The old system, in which the US kept the Middle East under control through military, political and economic links, is just about finished. The ground is shifting under everyone's feet, so that in their different ways both Saudi Arabia and Israel are now out in the cold and Shia Islam is in the ascendant. A new alliance with Sunni Islam is up for grabs.

In Iran, the big winner after the deal is President Rowhani. He is affable, moderate and calm and has managed to stabilise the country after the violent ups and downs of the Ahmadinejad years. Any reformist leader can rely on roughly two-thirds of the electorate for support but the complexities of the Iranian constitution and the wiles of the politicians have often shackled the reformists' powers. Now, however, the wave of prosperity that ought to follow the lifting of sanctions should strengthen Rowhani greatly. Will he be able to convert this into new political powers?

For those of us in the west, there are immediate, practical advantages. Iran's oil will be back on the open market and should drive the price of oil down to $50 or maybe even lower: a big economic benefit. Whatever we may think of Iran, relying on prejudice and the television pictures of angry crowds, the reality is that the country is a sophisticated society that can once again play the pivotal role it did under the shah—though, one hopes, with a bit more common sense.

Is the world safer now? Not particularly, if only because the threat from Iran was mostly exaggerated out of proportion by Israel and the American right. Yet it will be a differently dangerous place. Sanctions, which are an unpleasant and lazy way of exercising power, have proven their effect; so has working with Russia instead of against it. The Vienna agreement will bring nothing good for Isis and it will be easier to co-ordinate a western/Shia campaign against it. The great anxiety now is felt by Saudi Arabia. What does it do and where does it go? After all the years of worrying about Iran, maybe we should start worrying about the Saudis instead?

Iran Can Still Have Nuclear Capability Within Two Decades

Blaise Misztal

Though the intention of the Iran nuclear deal is to prevent Iran from developing nuclear weapons, even President Obama realized that it wouldn't prevent that indefinitely. In this viewpoint, Blaise Misztal, director of the Bipartisan Policy Center's national security program, explains with the aid of several helpful charts, how Iran can, over the next few years, gradually lay the groundwork for a nuclear weapon without violating the terms of the agreement, and he calculates exactly how long it will be before Iran can make that move, even if it sticks to the terms of the agreement.

In defending the April 2 framework agreement that laid the foundation for the final nuclear deal with Iran, President Obama admitted that one of its chief weaknesses, and one of his main concerns, was that, "in year 13, 14, 15, they have advanced centrifuges that enrich uranium fairly rapidly, and at that point the breakout times would have shrunk almost down to zero."

In the text of the final deal, known as the Joint Comprehensive Plan of Action (JCPOA), it is possible to identify the specific provisions the president was likely referring to (Sections F, G, I, and K of Annex I), and understand how they might allow Iran to work up to the edge of a nuclear weapons capability, legally, and calculate when Iran might reach such capability.

"Can Iran Gain Nuclear Weapons Capability While Complying with the Deal?" by Blaise Misztal, Bipartisan Policy Center, August 3, 2015. Reprinted by Permission.

It turns out that, even if Iran were to honor all of its obligations and fully comply with all the restrictions in the JCPOA, the deal would not prevent a nuclear Iran indefinitely. Starting in year 13, Iran will be able to breakout (produce enough fissile material for a nuclear weapon) in about 10 weeks, down from one year. But it would not be until year 16—later than President Obama's initial assumption—that Iran would attain nuclear weapons capability and a breakout time of less than 3 weeks.

Nuclear Weapons Capability and Breakout

There are three main elements of a nuclear weapon: fissile material, the explosive device that starts a nuclear chain reaction using the fissile material (known as the weapon), and a delivery mechanism. Of these, the first is the most difficult to master and easiest to observe. For this reason, although a country is not a known nuclear power until it conducts a successful test detonation of a nuclear device, a country is assumed to have a nuclear weapons capability once it is believed to be capable of producing enough fissile material for a weapon. At that point, a state could already possess the knowhow to put the fissile material into a weapon and a delivery vehicle, putting it a potential "turn of a screwdriver" away from possessing a working nuclear bomb. In other words, there is a difference between when a country will start being treated like a nuclear power by others (when it has the fissile material for a nuclear weapon) and when it becomes a nuclear power (when it actually tests a working weapon).

The critical question is how quickly can enough fissile material be produced for a nuclear weapon, commonly referred to as a "breakout"? Related questions are: would it be possible to detect production of fissile material before the task is completed? And can any such attempted breakout be stopped? The JCPOA seeks to keep Iran from gaining a nuclear weapons capability by putting in place, for a certain amount of time, restrictions that would mean any attempted breakout would take at least a year, requiring inspections that would detect such a breakout promptly, and creating a mechanism to punish Iran if it does cheat on the deal and attempt to develop a nuclear weapons capability.

Assuming the deal works as intended during its term, the major issue is what will happen to Iran's breakout timing once the JCPOA's restrictions begin to expire. Proponents of the deal point out that the inspections and monitoring regime will remain intact, some of it indefinitely. But should Iran's ability to produce fissile material ever exceed the detection capacity of the inspections, it will have effectively achieved nuclear weapons capability.

It is impossible to fully determine how quickly Iran might be able to breakout in the future or how quickly inspectors might be able to detect any such move, but some general assumptions and calculations can be made that give a rough idea of that timeline:

First, what breakout timing could outpace detection and prevention? One year seems to be enough, based on the comfort of the United States with that timeline as enshrined in the JCPOA. Even a two- to three-month window seems acceptable, as keeping Iran at that distance was the stated objective of the interim Joint Plan of Action agreed to in November 2013. The tipping point seems to arrive around one month. The JCPOA puts in place a 30-day long dispute resolution process—where the United States or other parties to the deal can confront any Iranian cheating. It would follow that world powers would have difficulty confronting and rolling back any Iran breakout that could occur faster than that. Thus, we will assume that to acquire nuclear weapons capability, Iran would need a breakout ability of roughly four weeks or faster.

Second, at what point might Iran have the capability to breakout in four weeks or less? Numerous variables affect how long breakout might take—primarily the number and efficiency of centrifuges being used as well as the amount and enrichment level of the starting uranium feedstock—but we can look to the administration's own judgment for guidance. Numerous U.S. officials have stated that the JCPOA is designed to keep Iran's breakout timing at one year. That means that the U.S. government has calculated that with the nuclear infrastructure Iran will be permitted to retain under the deal—5,060 IR-1 centrifuges and 300 kilograms of 3.5 percent enriched uranium—it would take 12 months to produce enough highly-enriched uranium for a nuclear weapon. Assuming that Iran's enriched uranium stockpile remains constant at 300 kilograms, we can calculate that, to be able to breakout in four weeks or less, Iran would need to have an enrichment capability equal to 13 times more IR-1 centrifuges (65,000 IR-1s) than it has now.

But what if Iran's stockpile of enriched uranium were to grow? Here, too, U.S. government statements can serve as a guide. Under the terms of the interim Joint Plan of Action (JPOA), Iran was allowed to operate roughly 9,000 centrifuges and more than enough 3.5 percent enriched uranium to produce fissile material for a nuclear device. Statements by government officials suggest that they believe that Iran's breakout timing under the JPOA would be roughly two to three months. Taking the more conservative estimate, we can calculate that, starting with a sufficient stockpile of 3.5 percent enriched uranium (about 1,800 kilograms), Iran would need roughly 30,000 IR-1 centrifuges to be able to breakout in four weeks or less.

Knowing this, the question of whether or when Iran might reach nuclear weapons capability under the JCPOA can be refined as follows:

Is there a point in the lifetime of the JCPOA at which Iran would be permitted to have, while remaining compliant with the terms of the deal, either:

a) An enrichment capacity equivalent to 65,000 IR-1 centrifuges and at least 300 kilograms of 3.5 percent enriched uranium

b) An enrichment capacity equivalent to 27,000 IR-1 centrifuges and around 2,000 kilograms of 3.5 percent enriched uranium

Answering that question will require examining the terms of the JCPOA itself.

Restrictions on Iran's Nuclear Program Under JCPOA

Three key restrictions, and their expiration dates, dictate when Iran might approach a nuclear weapons capability under the terms of the JCPOA—number of centrifuges operating, type of centrifuges operating, and size and enrichment level of Iran's enriched uranium stockpile.

Centrifuge Operation

Under the JCPOA, Iran is, at first, only allowed to enrich uranium in 5,060 centrifuges located at the underground Natanz Fuel Enrichment Plant. During this period, the operational centrifuges are required to be the IR-1 model, the same antiquated model based on designs purchased from Pakistan's A.Q. Khan that Iran has been using for enrichment for the last 12 years.

However, the number of centrifuges at Natanz is only limited for the first decade. And given that the facility is designed to hold 50,000 centrifuges, constraining Iranian enrichment to Natanz between years 10 and 15 will have no significant effect on the scope of that activity.

Thus, 10 years into the deal, Iran will be able to begin expanding its enrichment program beyond just 5,060 centrifuges. That expansion will not be unlimited, at least so long as Iran maintains its obligations under this deal. Instead it will be governed by a long-term plan that Iran will have to submit to the International Atomic Energy Agency (IAEA) as part of its compliance with the JCPOA. But even without the public release of this plan, other parts of the deal hint at how much enrichment capacity Iran will gain and how quickly it will do so.

Advanced Centrifuges

While JCPOA might limit the centrifuges Iran can use to enrich uranium for the first decade, it does allow for the continuation of research into more advanced centrifuge models and even their production in large quantities. For the first eight years of the deal, Iran is allowed to enrich uranium for research purposes, but immediately dilute the product so as not to accumulate any additional enriched uranium, in small quantities of IR-4, IR-5, IR-6, and IR-8 centrifuges. After this period it will be allowed to expand its testing of IR-6 and IR-8 centrifuges to up to 30 machines of each type.

This larger scale testing is clearly so that these next-generation centrifuges will replace the IR-1 in Iran's enrichment facilities. JCPOA accepts that "Iran will begin phasing out its IR-1 centrifuges in 10 years" (Par. 2) as well as that "Iran will begin to install necessary infrastructure for the IR-8 at Natanz…after year 10." (Annex I, Sec. I, Par. 53) In anticipation of this switch over from the IR-1, JCPOA even allows Iran to get a head start in producing a stockpile of IR-6 and IR-8 centrifuges for future use. Beginning in year nine, the deal allows Iran to manufacture 200 machines of each model, at first without all the necessary parts put together and then, after year 10, fully assembled (Annex I, Sec. K, Par. 63).

Moving Iran's production of enriched uranium to these next-generation models is significant because of how much more effective they will be at this task. Pinning down the performance of the IR-6 and IR-8 machines can be tricky as there is no real data to analyze yet, but a comparison can be made to the IR-1. The IR-6 is actually a slightly larger version of the IR-2m that Iran currently has installed, but is not operating, at Natanz. This model is commonly reported to be roughly five times as fast as the IR-1. The IR-8, on the other hand, has been described by Iranian officials as capable of enriching uranium 17 times faster than the IR-1. Thus, the 200 centrifuges of each of the IR-6 and IR-8 models that Iran will be allowed to produce after year eight, actually represent the equivalent enrichment capability of an additional 4,400 IR-1 centrifuges *each year*.

What is not specified in the text of the JCPOA, contained instead in the separate plan Iran will file with the IAEA, is when these advanced centrifuges would be allowed to start enriching uranium. We know that it will not be before year 11—restrictions on number and type of operational centrifuges, as well as stockpiling enriched uranium produced in IR-6 and IR-8 centrifuges, remain in effect for 10 years. But at what point after that and at what rate Iran will be permitted to begin installing the centrifuges it began building in year nine remains unclear. Based on the comments made by President Obama—that the worry of a quick breakout only begins to emerge in year 13—it would seem that the IR-6 and IR-8 centrifuges would not be switched on immediately after year 10, but would begin enriching before year 15.

Enriched Uranium Stockpile

The final piece of the breakout time equation is the size and enrichment level of the starting feedstock. Enriching natural uranium to 3.5 percent actually takes longer than enriching from 3.5 to 90 percent (weapons grade). That is why the JCPOA imposes significant limits on the amount of 3.5 percent enriched uranium that Iran is allowed to keep on hand. By ensuring that it does not have enough of it to produce enough fissile material for a nuclear device, the deal prolongs the breakout timing.

Specifically, Iran is permitted to stockpile only 300 kilograms of 3.5 percent enriched uranium for the first 15 years of the deal. After that period, both the limit on the size of Iran's stockpile and its enrichment level lapse. (Annex I, Sec. E, Par. 25; Sec. F, Par. 28; Sec. J, Par. 56) Even with just the minimum of 5,060 IR-1 centrifuges, Iran will be capable of producing between 1,500 and 2,000 kilograms of 3.5 percent enriched uranium in a year. And with the additional enrichment capability it will gain from the IR-6 and IR-8 centrifuges, its total annual 3.5 percent enriched uranium output is likely to be much higher. Thus, by the end of year 16 Iran will have at least 1,800 kilograms of 3.5 percent uranium, enough for a nuclear device, significantly reducing its breakout timing.

Estimating Breakout Timing

With the above information, it is possible to begin calculating when, under the terms of JCPOA, Iran might gain a nuclear weapons capability. There are two scenarios in which Iran might see its breakout time drop below the four weeks we assume to be the threshold it would need to reach for nuclear weapons capability.

The first scenario, in which Iran's stockpile of 3.5 percent enriched uranium remains at 300 kilograms, would require Iran to acquire the equivalent of 65,000 IR-1 centrifuges to reach nuclear weapons capability. Given that it will already have 5,060 of those installed, the question is how long it would take Iran to install the equivalent of another 60,000 IR-1s. Given that we know Iran will be producing the equivalent of roughly 4,400 IR-1 centrifuges a year in the form of IR-6 and IR-8 machines, we can calculate that it would take almost 14 years after manufacturing of the advanced centrifuges began to produce the necessary enrichment capability. Under this first scenario, Iran would acquire nuclear weapons capability 22 years (an eight year restriction on building advanced centrifuges followed by 14 years to acquire enough of them) after JCPOA goes into effect.

In the second scenario, Iran lowers its breakout timing to 4 weeks or less by increasing its 3.5 percent enriched uranium feedstock to roughly 1,800 kilograms and installing the equivalent of 30,000 IR-1 centrifuges. We know that the restriction on the size of Iran's enriched uranium lapses in year 15, that it will already have a stockpile of 300 kilograms of 3.5 percent enriched uranium, and that at minimum it will be able to produce 1,500 kilograms of 3.5 percent enriched uranium a year. That means that by the end of year 16, Iran will have at least the 1,800 kilograms of 3.5 percent enriched uranium that is required under this scenario. But will it have the equivalent of 30,000 centrifuges installed by then? Given that Iran will begin producing the equivalent of 4,400 IR-1 centrifuges annually after year eight, by year 16 it will have added the equivalent of 35,200 IR-1 centrifuges, more than enough enrichment capability than required under this scenario, even if the original 5,060 IR-1 centrifuges are removed. Under the second scenario, Iran would acquire a nuclear weapons capability

16 years after JCPOA goes into effect, at which point its breakout timing would be less than 3 weeks.

It turns out that President Obama was right in his general assertion, although perhaps overly pessimistic in his calculations: JCPOA does not prevent a nuclear Iran indefinitely; Iran's breakout window drops precipitously sometime between years 10 and 15 of the deal; but Iran will attain nuclear weapons capability while remaining fully compliant with the JCPOA, just after 16 years, not 13 as predicted by the president.

In fact, the Obama administration had argued for keeping in place the stronger prohibitory language of Resolution 1929, but it lost that argument when its negotiating partners wouldn't back the Americans up.

"When Mr. Obama sought to include a prohibition on ballistic missiles in the Iran deal, or at least extend a previous Security Council resolution banning them, not just Russia and China but even our European allies in the nuclear negotiations refused," former Obama White House official Philip Gordon explained this week in the *New York Times*. "They argued that the ballistic missile ban was put in place in 2010 only to pressure Iran to reach a nuclear deal, and they refused to extend it once that deal had been concluded."

The question remains, what next? In a short briefing paper on Iran's missile testing, analysts at the Iran Project, a non-governmental group including former diplomats say the challenge for President Trump is to "constrain Iran's missile testing while maintaining the U.S. and Iranian commitment to the JCPOA, the most assured way to prevent Iran from acquiring a nuclear weapon."

The Security Council scheduled "urgent consultations" on Iran's missile test earlier this week.

Gordon, the former White House official, noted that Iranian presidential elections this spring will likely prompt hardliners to stake out a position of defiance in the missile dispute. The stage would seem to be set for tough rhetoric to escalate, he wrote, including the possibility of terrorist attacks on Americans in the Mideast.

The Oil Won't Start Flowing Immediately

Brad Plumer

So far in this chapter, you've been reading about how close Iran is to gaining nuclear weapons, and how a nuclear-armed Iran might affect the balance of power in the Middle East and possibly increase the chances of nuclear war. However, the other side of the question is how removing economic sanctions against Iran can affect both Iran's economy and that of the United States (and most of the rest of the world as well). In the following viewpoint, Brad Plumer, senior editor at Vox Media, discusses the potential effect of the JCPOA on oil prices.

From an economic standpoint, one of the most significant aspects of today's US-Iran nuclear deal is that it could open up Iran's vast crude oil reserves to the rest of the world. Once Europe and the US ease their sanctions, Iran can ramp up crude production and exports, locking in this new era of low oil prices.

But here's the catch—this won't all happen immediately. It will likely take at least six months before we see any significant oil impact from the deal, and possibly even longer than that.

Even if all goes according to plan, the US and EU won't lift sanctions on Iran until 2016 at the earliest. Once that happens, Iran can finally start selling some of the roughly 30 to 40 million barrels of oil it currently has stored in vast floating tankers off its coast. That could help push oil prices down moderately.

But after that, it might take years for Iran to get production in its crippled oil fields back to pre-sanctions levels. The country does possess vast crude reserves—but that doesn't mean it's all coming online tomorrow.

Iran has the world's fourth-largest oil reserves—but sanctions have crippled output

Iran is sitting on some 158 billion barrels of crude oil, the fourth-largest proved reserves in the world. But thanks to a slew of sanctions by the United States and Europe in recent years—meant to pressure Iran over its nuclear program—the nation's oil fields have fallen into serious decline, driven by a lack of investment.

Back in 2008, Iran produced some 4 million barrels of oil per day. By May 2015, that had fallen to just 2.8 million barrels per day. (To put that in perspective, the entire world uses about 90 million barrels of oil per day, so this is a significant amount.)

Iran currently has 30 to 40 million barrels of oil stored at sea

On top of that, Iran has been having trouble selling the oil that it *can* still pump out—particularly after the EU imposed sanctions in 2012 that barred insurers from covering ships that carry Iranian oil.

Iran's exports plummeted from 2.6 million barrels per day in 2011 down to 1.4 million barrels per day in 2014—with sales going mainly to China, India, Japan, South Korea, and Turkey. [...]

The rest is just ... sitting there. Iran has been storing much of the oil that it can't export on massive floating tankers off its coast. Most estimates suggest they have around 30 to 40 million barrels in storage, with about half of that crude oil and the other half condensates.

This, in theory, should be the first effect of the Iran deal. Once sanctions are lifted, this stored oil can get sold off. The key question is how quickly this will all happen.

Sanctions won't be lifted for at least six months

So now comes the US-Iran nuclear deal, in which Iran gives up the bulk of its nuclear program in exchange for sanctions relief. In theory, that will allow Iran to boost oil exports and production.

But it will be at least six months before sanctions start getting lifted—and even that might be optimistic. Richard Nephew, a former State Department official who served as lead sanctions expert for the US team negotiating with Iran, explains the timeline here:

> *First, the agreement involves an extensive procedure for ascertaining the support of home legislative and other legal bodies for it. In the US system, this will take at least 30–60 days as Congress will need to receive the text of the deal, hold hearings on it, and decide what to do. ....*
>
> *Second, the implementation will itself take months. Iran's list of nuclear steps is long, as is appropriate considering they are the party in need of building the most confidence. I've noted for a long time that removal and storage of centrifuges will be the long-pole in the timing tent, and nothing in the text contradicts this. Based on the schedule in the document, all of this work will not even start until after 90 days from today (the end of October) and it will take months from that point to fully execute the remaining changes to Iran's nuclear program.*
>
> *Third, sanctions relief itself will not flow until these nuclear steps are completed. There will be meetings and business trips by trading companies, investment firms, and by oil companies and potentially even concluded contracts (if not signed until the deal comes into force). But, if these steps cross the sanctions line, the Obama Administration has made clear that it will be forced to act. Iran will not and cannot obtain relief without having completed its part of the bargain.*

So Iran shouldn't expect sanctions relief until the first half of 2016—and possibly even later than that, if implementation ends up getting bogged down in mistrust or other disputes.

Even after sanctions are lifted, Iran could struggle to boost production

Once sanctions are lifted, Iran has several options. First, it can start selling all that oil it has sitting in offshore tankers. Iran probably won't want to unload this *all* at once (since that could cause prices to crash), but the International Energy Agency estimates that it could sell some 180,000 barrels per day for six months.

Those sales would bump up global crude supplies modestly, although they're unlikely to upend oil markets on their own. (That said, we might see other countries increase their own production in response to these sales, as they fight to maintain market share. That would push prices down further.)

After that, Iran will likely try to bolster production in some of its existing fields, although it's unclear how much is actually possible. The IAEA estimates that Iran will be able to increase oil production from its current level of 2.8 million barrels per day to around 3.5 million barrels per day "within months of sanctions being lifted."

But Nephew, for his part, is skeptical that Iran can ratchet up production that quickly. For one, he says, Iran is facing "fatigued fields and antiquated equipment." Once pumping ceases in a field, it's not so simple to just flip a switch and turn it back on. By some estimates, Iran will need $50 billion to $100 billion in foreign investment to get production back up to pre-sanctions levels. That could take years.

What's more, Nephew points out, foreign investors are likely to be wary about rushing into Iran. "Iran itself is a difficult environment in which to work," he writes. "The Iranian bureaucracy is formidable and it will be a real achievement if the Iranian government is able to deliver on its bait to international oil companies and others to make the process less painful."

Plus, there's always the risk that the nuclear deal falls through and the United States and Europe reimpose sanctions: "Sanctions snap-back is a real threat and businesses would be well-advised to design their contracts with Iran accordingly. Companies and banks that develop business ties in Iran will need to be prepared to have them vacated immediately if Iranian cheating is detected."

Bottom line: The IAEA thinks Iran can get back to producing 4 million barrels of oil per day—the level it was at in 2008—by the end of this decade. Oil Minister Bijan Namdar Zangeneh wants Iran to resume its spot as the world's No. 2 oil exporter behind Saudi Arabia (a spot currently occupied by Russia). But that's far from assured, and there could easily be hiccups on the way.

What would more Iranian oil mean for the United States? Lower gas prices, for one.

If Iran *can* ramp up oil production in the coming years, that would put downward pressure on global oil prices, which in turn could be a big deal for the United States.

Global crude oil prices have already fallen from $115 per barrel last June to around $58 per barrel today—a major storyline for the global economy. That price crash, in turn, has pushed down gasoline prices and made driving cheaper for Americans, freeing up money to spend on other things.

On the flip side, low prices have *also* squeezed US oil companies working in costly shale regions like North Dakota and Texas. Over the past year, drillers have responded to lower prices by slashing costs and steadily improving efficiency—and US oil production has held surprisingly steady. But fresh competition from Iran will make this task even tougher.

That said, the Iran story is likely to unfold over several years—it won't happen right away. It's telling that oil prices didn't drop in the day after the US-Iran nuclear agreement was announced. One explanation is that traders had been expecting a deal for months and they'd already priced in its effects. But another explanation is that it will take time for Iranian oil to reach the market, and nothing's guaranteed just yet.

Iran's Energy Production Faces Challenges

Thomas W. O'Donnell

In the following viewpoint, Thomas W. O'Donnell, an energy consultant who teaches at the Free University and Hertie School of Governance in Berlin, explains how Iran expanded its energy production faster than most analysts expected. However, he points out that to significantly increase oil production and sustain that increase, Iran needs foreign technology and investment, yet that is not happening to the degree necessary. That, O'Donnell argues, is due not so much to economic considerations as internal policies and politics in Iran.

Since the Obama-administration's and Europe's nuclear sanctions were lifted early this year, Iran has been expanding its production and exports more rapidly than most experts had expected. Tehran has actually tripled exports since late-2015. But, here's the big question: Can Iran sustain this years' production gains?

If to, this could seriously undermine Saudi Arabia's global oil-market share, and boost Iran's sanctions-damaged economy to a long-awaited recovery.

The short answer: Now that foreign sanctions are finally lifted, the battle to boost Iran's oil exports has shifted to a domestic clash over whether to allow foreign oil companies to have significant upstream involvement. This is a domestic Iranian issue with a long history.

"What's keeping foreign oil firms out of Iran? IRG?" by Thomas W. O'Donnell, The Global Barrel, June 17, 2016. Reprinted by Permission.

Iranian Crude Oil Production

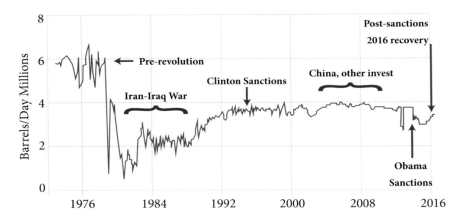

To put Iran's recent production increases in perspective: On its own, for 37 years, Iran has struggled to produce two-thirds of its pre-revolutionary level of 6 million barrels/day. Now, domestic opposition is again limiting foreign oil companies' participation to boost production.

Historical perspective

Let's start with some historical perspective: The Iranian National Oil Company (NIOC) can only do so much on its own to boost production. After decades of sanctions, it lacks the needed technology and finance. I told CNNMoney's Matt Egan, on Wednesday, that the faster Iran expands *on its own*, the faster production will plateau.

This was what happened after the 1980–1988 Iran-Iraq war. By about 1992, production had plateaued at almost 4 million barrels/day, under ⅔ of the pre-revolutionary, late-1970's level of roughly 6 million barrels per day. The Iranian president at the time, Rafsanjani, argued to religious conservative and nationalist members of the Majilis that only foreign oil companies' technology and investments could expand production further. However, he only won grudging approval for an offshore project due to fears that foreigners would bring their irreligious ways ashore and/or undermine the hard-won nationalization of Iran's oil sector.

But then, in May 1995, Bill Clinton imposed the first US sanctions on Iran's oil sector due to Tehran's nuclear program. And, as can be seen from the chart, over the next 20-plus years, Iranian production has never gone much higher as it experienced varying degrees of sanctions and periods of foreign investment by Chinese and western firms.

Today

Now, coming back to the present, today's leadership of Iran's national oil company is also painfully aware of what Rafsanjani realized at the end of the Iran-Iraq War: To increase production significantly above two-thirds of the pre-revolution level, the sector urgently needs to attract foreign oil companies' technology and investments on a large scale.

In fact, international oil companies (IOCs) have been anxiously anticipating these opportunities since well before it was clear a nuclear deal would be signed. Iranian oil is very cheap to get out of the ground and thus inherently very competitive even in this low-price market. This makes Iran a place the IOCs would love to invest to offset the big investment cuts they have had to make in higher-cost projects since prices fell.

Domestic opposition

So, what is the holdup? On this point, my comments to CNN differ from those by other experts [...]. Those who spoke with Bloomberg attributed the slowness to foreign companies' reticence about running afoul of some remaining US sanctions, which prohibit dealing with Iran in US dollars.

Indeed, dollars can be an issue, but, with all due respect (esp. to Dan Yergin), the IOC's have lots of experience dealing successfully with such restrictions in various countries—as long as it's legal to be working in the given country. So, this is hardly a deal breaker.

This all begs the question: why have the details of new contract provisions not been forthcoming from Tehran for so long now?

As I indicated to CNN, this has to do with internal Iranian policy clashes, between factions having conflicting economic interests. In particular, academic experts report that the Revolutionary Guards have had a lucrative business under sanctions contracting with the INOC for oil-field service work. And, they are not inclined to let themselves become exposed to competition from highly capable international firms. So, they have blocked agreement on new contract terms that would permit more foreign involvement. In this, it is easy for them to opportunistically play the nationalist card. And, there remains in Iran significant opposition from religious conservatives and nationalists who oppose any foreign upstream participation, esp. foreigners owning oil reserves in any form.

Here is a case, not unusual in Iran, of a corrupt faction putting its own narrow economic interests over the national interests. The nation's interests clearly favor seizing the opportunity presented by the end of export sanctions to attract foreign investment for rebuilding the oil sector and boosting exports while the time is ripe in the market to do so.

(Aside: Failure to do so now, when Iran has a competitive advantage with its low-cost reserves, could stall its oil-production recovery for many years hence. In this, the mullahs running the country can take an object lesson from Venezuela. There, a decade or more ago, Hugo Chavez turned away the many foreign companies that were then happy to pay top dollar to develop Venezuela's extra-heavy oil in the Faja Orinoco. He even gave the Chinese a very hard time to invest (as opposed to loaning money for oil deliveries due years later). And then came the US fracking revolution and then came low prices and now no-one wants to make big investments in upgraders for extra-heavy oil. So too, Iran's unique moment might soon have passed.)

Where are Iran's long-promised new-contract details?

It is well know that foreign companies have been waiting to see the INOC's long-promised new contract terms. There has been repeated disappointment with what has been offered till now. I am told by companies involved that, in each instance, the details have been both exasperatingly thin and not so different from the old pre-sanctions "buy-back" contracts which all sides agree will no longer work.

(Aside 2: For a brief explanation of how the old buy-back contracts prohibited foreign ownership of upstream resources and restricted investments, see the EIA's Iran country analysis, written a full year ago, back in June 2015, which already said: "Iran is planning to change its oil contract model to allow IOCs to participate in all phases of an upstream project, including production." Meanwhile, sanctions blocking Iranian exports have been lifted since January of this year, and the promised new foreign-participation contract details are still unclear.

Future

It'll be interesting to see how this plays out. If the Iranians don't get domestic agreement on their contract terms solidified ... and offer terms that are sufficiently appealing to the big foreign firms they need to attract for long-term projects, their present production expansion will stall, at best, at the same level it always has since the Revolution 37-years ago: around 4 million barrels per day.

That would be good news for the Saudis and ambitious Prince Mohammad, but not good for Iranians generally who are weary of their years-long depressed economy and the domestic political and economic dysfunction under the rule of the mullahs.

The Future of US-Iran Relations

Preface

As we saw in the two previous chapters, the relationship between Iran and the United States goes back many years, but events in the late twentieth and early twenty-first centuries have been quite dramatic. In this chapter, you will read viewpoints that examine the potential future effects of recent developments between the two nations. Of course, the relationship between any two nations is not limited to just those two. In the case of the United States and Iran, Israel has a major stake in the outcome of any negotiations between the two.

The first viewpoint, written before the Iran deal was approved, focuses on how even though Israel strongly opposed the deal, it might, in the end, give Israel and its supporters more influence in the region and in Washington. Other viewpoints examine what trade might look like between the two nations after sanctions are lifted and what the foreign policy of a truly moderate and open Iran might look like.

However, despite the promise offered by the nuclear deal, relations between Iran and the United States suffered an enormous setback when newly elected US president Donald Trump signed an executive order banning Iranians (as well as people from several other Middle Eastern nations) from entering the United States. Several of the viewpoints in this chapter examine the potential effects of this ban on students, scholars, and scientists in the United States and Iran, as well as the effect on science and scholarship worldwide.

In many of the articles in this chapter, you will not only learn the views of the author, but get a glimpse into the lives and voices of many Iranians and Iranian-Americans, further demonstrating that while the issues that surround the relationship between Iran and the United States are indeed complex and require caution as well as an honest and open dialogue among members of both nations, it is in the best interests of the citizens of each nation that the issues be faced and dealt with.

As the chapter—and the book—closes, it is with the haunting notion that Iranians are moving forward, fighting against oppressive regimes, while Americans may very well be taking huge leaps backward. Changes in relations between America and Iran may come at a high price.

The Iran Nuclear Deal Could Actually Increase Israel's Influence

Daniel Wagner

Daniel Wagner, author and managing director of a DC-area risk-management firm, was firmly opposed to the Iran deal, even though a substantial majority of American Jews supported it. However, in this viewpoint, he concedes that—conditions in the Middle East being totally unpredictable—the deal poses potential benefits as well as risks to Israel. Conservatives in Israel and pro-Israel conservatives in the United States will have developed more lobbying skills in the process of debating the agreement, and a clever response to shifting powers and loyalties in the Middle East could also provide opportunities for Israel to increase its influence, he argues.

T he Iran nuclear deal poses colossal challenges to Israel on many levels, among them, how effectively Israel's voice is being heard in Washington and in the region. AIPAC [American Israel Public Affairs Committee] has made some excellent arguments about why the deal should not be approved by the U.S. Congress, citing the absence of anytime, anywhere short-notice inspections (which is how the Obama administration initially characterized the deal), a failure to make sanctions relief conditional on full Iranian cooperation with the IAEA, the absence of military site inspections, and that it gives the Iranians the ability to store most of its centrifuges, rather than destroy them. There's only

"How the Iran Deal May Impact Israel's Influence," by Daniel Wagner, The Huffington Post. Reprinted by Permission.

one problem—according to three recent surveys, most American Jews, and most Americans more generally, favor the agreement.

Before the Iran Deal was reached, 59 percent of American Jews supported the idea of agreement, and virtually the same number (60 percent) supported the deal after it was concluded, according to polls conducted with 1,000 adults who identified themselves as Jewish in June and July by J Street. This exceeds the percentage of overall adult Americans who support it (56 percent), according to a poll conducted by ABC News and the *Washington Post* immediately after the agreement was signed in Vienna. Given the agreement's numerous flaws (as noted above), one wonders how many of these people have actually read the agreement, understand it, and have thought critically about it. Presumably, very few.

In this Kafkaesque scenario, what chance do AIPAC and Israel have of successfully influencing Congress's vote? The short answer is, not as much as many would like to believe, for two reasons. First, it appears that AIPAC does not represent the views of the majority of American Jews. Of the approximately 5.5 million Jews in the U.S., fewer than 100,000 are members of AIPAC, and most appear not to identify with its conservative platform. Second, although AIPAC has punched very much above its weight with great impact for decades, whatever impact it may have on this particular issue through its hearty lobbying will be a byproduct of the domestic political dynamics accompanying the debate in Washington, rather than the driving force behind it.

Despite the polling, there is growing opposition to the Deal in Washington and around the country, and it appears likely that Congress will vote to reject the deal and that President Obama will override it. There is also a very real chance that Congress will override the override, as its details become more widely known among constituents, even though many political pundits don't see it that way at the present time. Regardless of how the vote plays out, Middle Eastern politics are likely to get even more complicated, but in the process, it may actually enhance AIPAC and Mr. Netanyahu's ability to influence the dialectic going forward.

IRAN DEAL COULD BE GOOD FOR TECH

The Iranian nuclear deal announced last week may have unexpected benefits for America's talent-hungry technology sector.

Iran has a robust and young population: around two-thirds of Iranians are under the age of 30. Millions of young Iranians are desperately underemployed, and have spent years honing the necessary skills to bypass Iran's strict controls on the Internet.

As a result, the average Iranian twentysomething is far likelier to know his way around proxy servers and other digital security tools than his American peers. This ease and know-how could be a boon to innovative companies seeking a strategic technological advantage.

With the new nuclear deal, the *Wall Street Journal* reports, U.S. tech firms may finally have a chance to recruit Iran's cleverest digital natives. A series of U.S. laws passed since Iran's 1979 revolution have discouraged American companies from hiring Iranian citizens at significant volume. The deal has the potential to roll back some of those restrictions.

Google and other Silicon Valley giants are already attracting graduates of top universities in Iran, including Sharif University and the University of Tehran. And young Iranians are just as eager to join major American companies. As one investor told the *Journal*, today's youth "all want to be Steve Jobs," not the Ayatollah Khomeini.

Current laws require the State Department to screen every single U.S. job candidate with Iranian citizenship, and determine whether they pose a threat to American security. But the nuke deal, and a gradually improving relationship between the West and Iran, could make that process easier over time—bringing the same hope to Iranian techies and European energy investors.

Americans of Iranian descent, many of whom migrated in the tumult of the revolution, have played a key role in the U.S. business landscape for years. It doesn't hurt that California is home both to America's tech industry and its biggest Iranian expatriate community. Prominent Iranian-Americans in science and technology today include Pierre Omidyar, who founded eBay.com, and NASA's famous "mohawk guy" Bobak Ferdowsi.

> Just like migrants from other highly educated countries like China, Russia and India, if they manage to win America's trust, Iranian tech workers have the potential to bring U.S. industry success for decades to come.
>
> —"How The Iran Deal Could Boost US Tech Companies," by Ivan Plis, The Daily Caller, July 20, 2015.

Whether the deal is rejected or not by the U.S. Congress, in the process, conservatives in Israel and in the U.S. will have enhanced their ability to flex their lobbying muscles going forward, and Israel will be well positioned to receive enhanced defense assistance from the U.S. The reason Israel should see a net benefit in that regard is because either the perceived threat from Iran's proxies will grow if the deal is approved, or U.S. lawmakers will want to grant Israel some defense 'sweeteners' should the deal not be approved, to make amends with Israel. The Iran deal masks the strength of the bilateral military relationship between Israel and the U.S., and whoever occupies the White House starting in 2017 should have a better relationship with the Israeli government than President Obama has had.

From a regional perspective, the Israeli government will certainly not change its tune if the deal is approved. The nascent threat from Iran will of course continue, and very likely worsen, as a result of Iran's enhanced ability to support its proxies throughout the region. Additional defensive weapons from America will no doubt prove useful over time. While Israel will likely see a net loss in terms of an even more hostile regional landscape, it will gain from its budding marriage of convenience with Saudi Arabia (which also vehemently opposes the deal, even though it will not publicly state so) and the other Gulf states which share a similar view of Iran. That dynamic will no doubt contribute to the tectonic shifts going on in the region, so Israel will not be left out of the equation. We should expect other 'unusual' regional alliances to emerge—both in favor and against Israel's interests—in time.

With the U.S. and Turkey finally making some military overtures in Syria, and with a pan-Arab military force having been utilized against the Houthis in Yemen, there is some reason to believe that the landscape may start to shift a bit more in Israel's favor, should those forces be used against Iranian interests in Syria and Iraq. But the political mosaic that is the Middle East is, and will remain, entirely unpredictable. There is as much chance that the Islamic State will grow in size and strength as that it will be defeated in the near term. At least Israel has the benefit of knowing that all the other parties are busy killing each other and that it is not the immediate target of the ongoing conflagration in the region. If Israel plays it cards right, its influence in Washington and the region could very well grow.

US Sanctions Against Iran Embolden Its Hardliners

Ali Seyedrazaghi

In the following viewpoint, Lancaster University Middle East researcher Ali Seyedrazaghi warns that President Donald Trump's position on Iran could undo everything accomplished by the nuclear deal and the more moderate government of President Hassan Rouhani—and thus give more power to Iran's conservative hardliners, causing further upheaval for Iranian citizens and Iran's relationship with America. One positive outcome: though the author of this piece feared for reformist president Hassan Rouhani's 2017 reelection prospects, he won by a landslide and vowed to continue battling sanctions against Iran.

The landmark nuclear deal struck in Vienna between Iran and a coalition of Western powers in 2015 aimed to reduce the global nuclear threat posed by Iran. In return for Iran accepting constraints on its nuclear programme, the P5+1 countries—the US, UK, France, China and Russia, plus Germany—and the European Union pledged to lift sanctions which had impoverished Iran for several decades.

A statement by former US president, Barack Obama, that Saudi Arabia would have to accept greater Iranian influence in the region as a result was also assumed to be a major policy shift for the US. But with the election of Donald Trump as president, this new power

"Iran's hardliners benefit from US ramping up talk of sanctions," by Ali Seyedrazaghi, The Conversation, May 15, 2017. https://theconversation.com/irans-hardliners-benefit-from-us-ramping-up-talk-of-sanctions-76439. Licensed Under CC-BY-ND 4.0 International.

TRUMP'S TRAVEL BAN IS A MONUMENTAL BLUNDER

On Friday, January 28, 2017, President Donald J. Trump made a monumental blunder by blocking all immigration from seven majority-Muslim countries and halting the flow of all refugees into the United States for 120 days. According to Trump, these policies will protect American citizens from Islamic terrorism. In reality, Trump's executive order will damage the reputation of the United States abroad and alienate the world's Muslim community of over one billion, causing immeasurable harm to American security.

The United States prides itself on being a hospitable country where people of all ethnicities and affiliations have a chance to thrive. By banning immigration from a handful of Muslim nations, Trump has undermined the values which America claims to stand for. Though the administration claims its ban is not religious but rather anti-terror, Trump's decision to place seven majority-Muslim countries on the blacklist certainly has religious connotations. Further, the ban has a clause suggesting that members of "minority religions" in the blacklisted nations be allowed entry. Essentially, this enables Christians and Jews from the seven banned nations to immigrate, while barring Muslims. Such a move is not only immoral but also threatens America's security by undermining the nation's image abroad. In order to hunt terrorists, enforce the law, and gather intelligence, the US is constantly cooperating with allies worldwide. By enacting xenophobic and widely-condemned policies, Trump has jeopardized America's reputation, which lessens the willingness of foreign informants and governments to assist the US.

The immigration ban will damage relations with two countries in particular: Iraq and Iran. Iraq is an American ally whose soldiers and citizens fight tirelessly against ISIS. By banning Iraqi citizens from entering the US, Trump has disrespected the people who tackle Islamic terror on a daily basis. As a result of the ban, America's counterterror operations in Iraq will be debased and American soldiers in Iraq may be targeted more intensely. Iran, for its part, has elected a relatively moderate president, and relations were improving to the point where Iran's nuclear program could be suppressed diplomatically. Instead of continuing to work with Iran, Trump has chosen to validate Iranians' fears that America is their enemy. It would not be surprising if Iran were to increase its militant activities and beef up its military pursuits in the wake of Trump's immigration ban.

Trump's order also halts the acceptance of all refugees for 120 days. To the citizens of countries which have absorbed millions of refugees, such as Turkey, this decision implies that the US is not willing to shoulder its share of the relocation burden. It also threatens America's image as a beacon of prosperity and safety for the world's displaced, a reputation America obtained by opening its arms to the world's displaced and persecuted.

Proponents argue that the ban could save multitudes of lives. However, it does not appear that Trump's executive action will reduce terror attacks at all. Immigrants from the seven nations Trump blacklisted, Iran, Iraq, Libya, Somalia, Sudan, Syria, and Yemen, are not particularly likely to become terrorists. In fact, the grand total of deaths caused by terrorists from the seven banned nations since 1975 is zero. The majority of Islamic terrorists hail from other nations, such as Saudi Arabia and Turkey, which are not included in the ban. For this reason, Trump's characterization of the ban as "anti-terror" has little merit.

Rather than reducing deaths to terrorist attacks, Trump's actions will likely have the opposite effect. Islamic terror thrives on the notion that America is "the enemy." When America shows compassion towards Muslims, Islamic terrorists have difficulty convincing people to fight the US. When America shows animosity and hatred towards Muslims, it is easy for groups such as ISIS to find recruits for their "jihad." American Muslims, many of whom are now separated from their friends and families by the ban, will feel persecuted and resentful, driving them into the arms of radical recruiters and likely increasing terrorist activities in the United States.

Of course, ensuring domestic security should be a priority of every administration. Unfortunately, Trump's executive order will have the opposite effect. By harming America's reputation and banning immigration from Muslim nations which do not present a significant threat, Trump has dealt a serious and lasting blow to America's security.

—"Trump's Immigration Ban Will Harm American National Security," by Alex Hempel, January 28, 2017, https://whitefleet.net/2017/01/28/trumps-immigration-ban-will-harm-american-national-security.

balance is under threat. A war of words between Washington and Tehran appears to reflect the new administration's view of Iran as a global threat rather than merely a regional troublemaker.

The previous administration's strategy was supposed to insulate the US from conflict in the Middle East—which Obama believed had nothing to do with America's national interest. The nuclear deal would also ideally bring some peace in the region between Iran, Saudi Arabia and Israel.

Iran signed the deal on the assumption that it would remove the military threat against Iran. In exchange for the International Atomic Energy Agency having more control over Iran's nuclear programme, Iran would keep a presence in the region, there would be a guarantee of security of the regime, and the US would lift sanctions against it.

But the new US administration appears to now want to again control the country's behaviour after Iran carried out a missile test and continued its support for Houthi rebels in Yemen. The US announced sanctions against companies and individuals suspected of being involved in Iran's nuclear programme, and suggested further pressure to come. As Trump himself tweeted:

> Donald J. Trump (@realDonaldTrump)
> "Iran is playing with fire - they don't appreciate how "kind"President Obama was to them. not me!"
> 7:28am- 3 Feb 2017

It is possible that Trump's policy will push Iran to conduct more ballistic missile tests, get involved more in Yemen and other new targets in the region, play a counterproductive role in Iraq and possibly increase its aggressive cyber programme.

Hard Times

Internally, securing the nuclear deal and improving Iran-US relations are President Hassan Rouhani's two biggest achievements, which he hopes to use in a campaign to get reelected in elections on May 19.

Despite the implementation of the deal, its impact on Iran's economy and Iranians' daily lives is not yet palpable. Iranians, who in the last few years put all their hopes for a better economic situation on the nuclear deal, are now facing an escalating rhetoric from the new US administration. Despite this, Rouhani has pledged to further improve Iran's relations with the West and even to remove the remaining sanctions, as a means of inviting foreign investment into the country and creating tangible economic change.

The immediate result of the rising tension now between the US and Iran is that it undermines Iranian moderates, including Rouhani's government, which put all their political capital in the deal in the lead up to this month's election. It is increasingly difficult for Rouhani to sell the deal to voters now given Trump's rhetoric.

Rouhani's hardliner competitors, Tehran's mayor, Mohammad Bagher Qalibaf, and Ebrahim Raisi, chairman of Astan Quds Razavi, one of the Muslim world's wealthiest charities, have concentrated their campaign on the economic problems, which Iranians have continued to face since the deal. So there is a real danger that hopeless and tired Iranians will do the same thing they did 12 years ago when Mahmoud Ahmadinejad became president through a vote for that populist hardliner.

Trump's foreign policy and the future of the Iran deal will play a significant role in Iran's presidential election. On the one hand there's Rouhani who is trying to convince voters and reassure the international community that the continuation of moderate government in Iran for the next four years will result in more integration of Iran in the global system and improve Iran's economy. On the other hand are the hardliners trying to change the outcome of the election by questioning the intangible result of the deal in light of escalating tension between Iran and the US.

It is true that regardless of what happens in the election, Iran will not alter its overall anti-Western outlook. But it is also arguable that the only chance to diffuse the tension between the West and Iran in the long term is for the moderates to stay in power.

Pushing the Iranian public towards hardliners is the probable outcome of a harsher US line. The threat of another populist and anti-Western administration in Iran is real and dangerous, in light of the economic hardship people are currently facing.

Trump's Muslim Ban Could Have a Chilling Effect on US Scholars

Elizabeth Redden

In the following viewpoint, you will see how President Trump's ban affected individuals—Iranians and US citizens alike— and especially higher education when it first took effect. Elizabeth Redden, a freelance writer and correspondent for Inside Higher Ed, speaks with several people affected by the ban and provides not only a political but human perspective on the issue. As Redden points out, many of those impacted by the ban are students, scholars, and researchers who have been here in the United States for some time.

An executive order signed by President Trump late Friday afternoon immediately barring immigrants and nonimmigrant visitors from seven Muslim-majority countries from entering the U.S. has had immediate effects on scholars and students. More than 17,000 students in the U.S. come from the seven countries affected by the immediate 90-day entry ban: Iran, Iraq, Libya, Somalia, Sudan, Syria and Yemen.

The American Civil Liberties Union reported late Saturday that a federal judge had granted its request to temporarily block the deportations of individuals from the seven countries who found themselves trapped in airports nationwide after the ban went into effect. The entry ban, however, remains in place.

"Stranded and Stuck," by Elizabeth Redden, Inside Higher Ed, January 30, 2017. Reprinted by Permission.

Trump's executive order only deals with entry to the U.S. It does not direct the removal of those already present, but it does mean that people who are lawfully present from the seven affected countries might not be able to get back into the country if they leave, even those who hold student visas that allow such travel.

One such student, Ali Abdi, tweeted Friday, "I am an Iranian Ph.D. student at Yale Uni. Now overseas to do research. Trump's EO [executive order] might prevent me from returning to the U.S.!"

Abdi, a fourth-year anthropology student, said in a Skype interview he traveled the weekend immediately following Trump's inauguration from New York to the United Arab Emirates to apply for a visa for Afghanistan, where he's doing his dissertation research.

"I still do not have a visa to go to Afghanistan," said Abdi, who for now remains in Dubai. "After the executive order signed by President Trump, it seems that all nationals of Iran and six other countries with Muslim-majority populations, they cannot go back to the U.S. if they are on student visas, work visas, or even if they are green card holders." (The administration initially applied the ban to green card holders before partially—but only partially—walking back on that Sunday and suggesting that lawful permanent residents would be admitted on a case-by-case basis "absent significant derogatory information indicating a serious threat to public safety and welfare." Most international students do not have green cards, but instead are on temporary, nonimmigrant student visas.)

"I also cannot go to Iran, my home country, because I am a human rights activist. I have been vocal against the injustices happening in my homeland over the past eight years since I left the country. So I'm in a situation that I am neither welcome by the Iranian government, nor by the American government," said Abdi.

"The American government doesn't let me in. The Iranian government lets me in. It doesn't let me out."

Abdi, who does hold a green card, was not sure when, if at all, he will be able to come back to the U.S.— and, given what's happened, his heart is not set on it. His original plan was to return to Yale after a year abroad to finish writing his dissertation and to graduate. He has already completed his classes and comprehensive exams.

"To be very honest with you, it's difficult for me to consider the U.S. as my home anymore, because it has a president now who is visibly racist, especially toward people coming from certain regions of the world, the Middle East and in particular Iran. I do not feel comfortable and safe and secure living there, compared to living in Dubai or living in Kabul," Abdi said.

He continued: "According to the Trump administration, the visa ban is supposed to make America safe again. It's interesting that the first few paragraphs of the executive order refer to Sept. 11. As we all know, the hijackers came from Saudi Arabia, Lebanon, Egypt and the U.A.E. None of those countries are on the list. I am not suggesting at all that the nationals of those countries should be banned—not at all, that is also bigotry, discrimination and racism—but what I'm saying is rather than being a way to make America safe and secure again, this executive order in my opinion is just a way to satisfy Iranophobic, Islamophobic and xenophobic sentiments that are on the rise in the United States."

The Executive Order

The executive order represents Trump's effort to follow through on his campaign pledge to temporarily suspend visa processing from certain countries "that have a history of exporting terrorism" and to put new, more "extreme" vetting procedures in place for those seeking visas. The order, framed as intended to prevent the entry of terrorists into the U.S., specifically references the risk that terrorists could enter on student or other forms of nonimmigrant visas, as well as through the refugee resettlement program.

The text of the order, republished by the *New York Times*, states: "Numerous foreign-born individuals have been convicted or implicated in terrorism-related crimes since Sept. 11, 2001, including foreign nationals who entered the United States after receiving visitor, student or employment visas, or who entered through the United States refugee resettlement program.

Deteriorating conditions in certain countries due to war, strife, disaster and civil unrest increase the likelihood that terrorists will use any means possible to enter the United States. The United States must be vigilant during the visa-issuance process to ensure that those approved for admission do not intend to harm Americans and that they have no ties to terrorism."

In addition to imposing the 90-day entry ban and directing a review and reform of visa procedures, the executive order calls for a 120-day suspension on all refugee admissions and an indefinite suspension on entry of all Syrian refugees. It orders that the U.S. admit no more than 50,000 refugees in fiscal year 2017, less than half the target of 110,000 set by the previous Obama administration.

Civil rights groups have condemned the executive order as a pretext for banning Muslims. Trump called at one point during the campaign for a "total and complete shutdown of Muslims entering the United States."

"I'm establishing new vetting measures to keep radical Islamic terrorists out of the United States of America," Trump said in signing the order. "We don't want 'em here. We want to ensure that we are not admitting into our country the very threats our soldiers are fighting overseas. We only want to admit those into our country who will support our country and love, deeply, our people."

The order is, however, already having deep effects on students and scholars who were already admitted into this country and suddenly found themselves unable to travel outside it for academic or personal purposes—if they want to be sure they can come back into the U.S., that is—or who were caught outside the country when the order was signed.

Stranded Students and Scholars

Payam Jafari is among those who finds himself stranded outside the country. He was planning to return to San Francisco on a Feb. 5 flight for his final semester in a master's program in filmmaking at the Academy of Art University after spending the winter break spent visiting his family in Iran. He said he has entered the U.S. four times in the past three years with no problems, and that his student visa is valid through November.

"I have spent three years of my life in San Francisco," Jafari said. "I've been working on my most important project in my life. It's going to be my first feature film. I've talked with professional actors, I have them interested in my project. I'm talking to an American and an Iranian-American—they're interested in investing in my project, and right now I don't know what to do."

"I'm in Iran," he said, "and my mind is in San Francisco."

Others prevented from entering the U.S. include Samira Asgari, an Iranian with a doctorate from Switzerland's École Polytechnique Fédérale de Lausanne, who told the *Boston Globe* she was turned away at the airport in Frankfurt. She was traveling to Boston to work on a project on tuberculosis at a Harvard University laboratory.

Nazanin Zinouri, a recent graduate of Clemson University's Ph.D. program in industrial engineering, was made to disembark a U.S.-bound plane in Dubai, U.A.E. Zinouri, who graduated from Clemson in August, had traveled to Iran about a week earlier to visit family. "No one warned me when I was leaving, no one cared what will happen to my dog or my job or my life there. No one told me what I should do with my car that is still parked at the airport parking. Or what to do with my house and all my belongings," Zinouri wrote in a widely shared Facebook post. "They didn't say it with words but with their actions, that my life doesn't matter. Everything I worked for all these years doesn't matter."

The University of Massachusetts reported that it was working to assist affected students, faculty and staff and that "several were out of the country at the time of the executive order, including two UMass Dartmouth faculty who were detained at Logan Airport on Saturday despite being lawful permanent residents of the U.S."

UMass Dartmouth reported Sunday that the two professors were released after three hours. "Now that our colleagues are safe," the interim chancellor, Peyton R. Helm, and provost, Mohammad Karim, said in a strongly worded statement, "we want to be clear that we believe the executive order does nothing to make our country safer and represents a shameful ignorance of and indifference to the values that have traditionally made America a beacon of liberty and hope."

The National Association of Graduate-Professional Students reported that Vahideh Rasekhi, a linguistics Ph.D. student and the president of the Graduate Student Union at the State University of New York at Stony Brook, was detained at New York's Kennedy Airport when she attempted to re-enter the U.S. and was not released until late Sunday afternoon. She had traveled abroad to renew her F-1 student visa, a 10-week process which she had recently completed.

Confusion and Concern

Significant confusion—including the contradictory guidance and implementation vis-à-vis green card holders—has marked the rollout of the order, which went into effect immediately after Trump signed it late Friday.

"What we have is, frankly, a matter of significant concern and a great deal of confusion and very little clarity," said Terry W. Hartle, senior vice president at the American Council on Education. "At this point it's clear that the executive order was issued without consulting the Departments of State, Homeland Security, Justice and Defense."

"Our hope here is [Homeland Security] will move pretty quickly to clarify the parameters of the order, and to define what it means for people in the United States, and people who are not in the United States who have valid visas. The big uncertainty for colleges and universities is what it means for students who are being admitted now for September. They'd need to get a new visa by August, and obviously new visas are going to be frozen for 90 days," Hartle said.

NAFSA: Association of International Educators issued a statement on Sunday strongly condemning the order as undermining America's safety and values of freedom, opportunity and openness.

"This is simply inconceivable," Esther D. Brimmer, NAFSA's executive director and CEO, said in the statement. "The latest executive order, egregious enough in its aim to suspend the refugee program and to enact a blanket ban on visa approvals from these seven nations and Syrian refugees fleeing violence, has also caused enormous collateral damage in its implementation. Universities and colleges have already begun reporting cases of students and scholars stranded after traveling for reasons including studying abroad, attending conferences and visiting sick or dying family members."

"This particular action took us away from policies, which, in the past, have made our nation safe and strong," Brimmer's statement continued. "Thoughtful policies and not those that are capricious and unpredictable have kept our country growing and thriving economically and educationally. Moreover, this action overlooks the balance between the openness that makes us great, with the security that keeps us safe. It ignores the careful and thorough vetting procedures that have been established to welcome who we want in our nation while keeping out those who intend us harm."

Peter McPherson, the president of the Association of Public and Land-grant Universities, said in a statement, "The impact of this decision goes beyond those immediately impacted. Our nation's universities are enriched and strengthened by the talent, insight and culture that international students, faculty, researchers and staff bring. With appropriate and effective vetting, international students from all countries and of all religions have long been a core part of our campus communities, and that should continue uninterrupted. We are also concerned that this decision adds great uncertainty to international students, researchers and others who might consider coming to our campuses."

A petition signed by more than 7,000 academics by early Sunday evening, including 37 Nobel laureates, condemns the entry ban as discriminatory based on religion and national origin and as detrimental to U.S. interests. The petition argues that the action by Trump damages the nation's position of leadership in higher education and research and poses an "undue burden" on certain international students and scholars.

"The people whose status in the United States would be reconsidered under this EO are our students, friends, colleagues and members of our communities," the petition states. "The implementation of this EO will necessarily tear families apart by restricting entry for family members who live outside of the U.S. and limiting the ability to travel for those who reside and work in the U.S. These restrictions would be applied to nearly all individuals from these countries, regardless of their immigration status or any other circumstances. This measure is fatally disruptive to the lives of these immigrants, their families and the communities of which they form an integral part. It is inhumane, ineffective and un-American."

Some university leaders also issued letters and statements about the changes. A particularly strong statement came from the University of Notre Dame's president, the Reverend John I. Jenkins, who called on Trump to rescind the order.

"The sweeping, indiscriminate and abrupt character of President Trump's recent executive order halts the work of valued students and colleagues who have already passed a rigorous, post-9/11 review process, are vouched for by the university and have contributed so much to our campuses. If it stands, it will over time diminish the scope and strength of the educational and research efforts of American universities, which have been the source not only of intellectual discovery but of economic innovation for the United States and international understanding for our world; and, above all, it will demean our nation, whose true greatness has been its guiding ideals of fairness, welcome to immigrants, compassion for refugees, respect for religious faith and the courageous refusal to compromise its principles in the face of threats," Father Jenkins said.

For International Students, "A Chilling Effect"

At Portland State University, which has 76 students from Iran, Iraq, Libya, Yemen and Syria, most of them graduate students,

President Wim Wiewel issued a statement describing the order as having "a chilling effect not only on these students but on our Muslim students and all international students."

"We have numerous students of Iraqi and Iranian origin," said Shabbir Abbas, the president of the Graduate Muslim Student Association at Rutgers University (and a U.S. citizen). "Firstly, they are heartbroken. Many of these students have come from war-ravaged and poverty-stricken nations. Coming here was not only a dream come true, but also something that required painstaking effort. Now with a few strokes of a pen it can all come crashing down."

"If they leave the country, their return is in doubt—actually, they won't be able to return—and a lot of these students, they have young children. They're in preschool, kindergarten," Abbas said.

One humanities Ph.D. student from Iran who asked not to be named described how the order has complicated—and potentially compromised—plans to travel overseas for dissertation research. The student, who just completed comprehensive exams, needs to travel to Europe, Turkey and Iran to conduct fieldwork and interviews and to visit museum collections and archives.

"I wanted to do it in summer of 2017, but now everything is just vague and I don't know what will happen," the student said.

Even if the ban were to be lifted in time for the summer, the student said, the entry ban has made it difficult to plan and to apply for funding to cover travel costs.

"When you want to do something like that, you have to plan ahead of time, you rent a place, you have a lot of things going on. It's not just like OK, in 90 days, if it's OK, I will go. No, you have to plan ahead of time. All your life is here."

"I just started writing grants for travel for scholarships and stuff like that to cover my expenses, to do the fieldwork that I'm going to do. I'm almost sure that they won't give it to me, just because they will feel like you're not going to be able to go, so they're going to give it to someone else."

Another Ph.D. student who did not want her full name used said that the ban could affect her summer plans to return to her home country of Iran to conduct field research and, after four long years, to see her family.

"I've been in a Ph.D. program for four years, and I haven't seen my family for the four years because I was so busy with all the course work," the student said. The promise of being able to see her family helped motivate her to do the work, she said. "I was telling myself, 'you're going to go back home and see your parents.'"

"My brother is getting married in the summer and the whole family wanted me to be there," the student said. When her mother heard the news of the entry ban, she "called me and she was crying," the student said. "She was asking, 'can you come back,' and I said, 'I don't think so in this situation.' And it was a horrible moment."

"This is unfair discrimination," the student said. "Why are they playing politics with students' lives? We're just students here, and we devoted our entire life to study, to have a better life, to find new things in the world, to just help humanity … We thought the United States is a country of freedom. It's a country of democracy and we're going to have a great education here; we're going to have a good life here, and we sacrificed being with our beloved ones, leaving our country just coming here with a hope to experience something democratic. We thought the government of the United States, they don't judge us based on our birthplace or based on our ethnicity or religion."

Iranians Are Wrongly Targeted by the Travel Ban

Golnaz Esfandiari

This viewpoint, also concerned with the Trump administration's ban on people from Iran (and other countries) entering the United States, was written by a journalist for Radio Free Europe and a native of Tehran, Golnaz Esfandiari. Here, Esfandiari points out, like in the previous viewpoint, that many of the people affected by this ban are students, scholars, and accomplished people who clearly pose no threat of terrorism. But she goes a bit further and criticizes the new president's understanding of the roots of terrorism and where recent terrorists have come from—mostly Saudi Arabia and Pakistan.

Anticipating an executive order from the White House to temporarily shut off Iranians' access to U.S. visas and other avenues to immigration, Iranians have voiced frustration with being targeted for exclusion alongside citizens from a handful of predominantly Muslim countries where conflicts are raging.

The prospect of such immigration curbs by U.S. President Donald Trump, a purported draft of which has circulated in U.S. media, appears to be roughly in line with Trump's campaign promise to impose security measures including at least a temporary ban on Muslims entering the United States in the face of a threat from "radical Islamic terrorism."

Iranians Raise Cry As They Brace For U.S. Immigration Ban", by Golnaz Esfandiari, Radio Free Europe/Radio Liberty, January 26, 2017. Reprinted by Permission.

The ban would come with a cloud also hanging over the fate of a major deal struck in 2015 between Tehran and world powers including the United States to limit Iran's nuclear program in exchange for sanctions relief. Trump has vowed to revisit that agreement, known as the Joint Comprehensive Plan of Action (JCPOA), which went into effect despite strident opposition from Iran hawks in the United States and hard-liners in Tehran.

Some Iranian-Americans were among vocal critics calling any visa and immigration ban on Iranians discriminatory and contrary to U.S. principles.

New York-based Mehdi Arabshahi, a former student activist jailed in Iran for his political activism, responded to reports that Trump would impose a minimum 30-day ban by asking whether visa restrictions would also apply for Academy Award-winning Iranian film director Asghar Farhadi, who was nominated for a second Oscar this week for his film *The Salesman*.

Tweeting from Iran, actress Taraneh Alidoosti, who plays the lead female role in *The Salesman*, called such a U.S. ban "racist" and said that she would not attend the Oscar ceremony in protest.

Los Angeles-based writer and arts curator Shiva Balaghi, a former professor of art history at Brown University, was also critical.

> Shiva Balaghi (@SBalaghi)
> "Born in Iran, have an EU passport, own a home in US, serve on university & museum boards in US? No US visa for you! #MuslimBan" 1:11pm-25 Jan 2017

Terrorist Tag

The U.S. Department of State designated Iran a "state sponsor of terrorism" in 1984, a view that is officially unchanged, and has reiterated more recently its accusation of "terrorist-related activity" by Tehran, including "support for Hizballah, Palestinian terrorist groups in Gaza, and various groups in Iraq and throughout the Middle East."

There was also criticism from inside Iran as the international community awaited word from the White House.

Ali, a 16-year-old student in Tehran who said he hoped to pursue a university degree in the United States in the future, told RFE/RL that the inclusion left him puzzled. "I don't understand why Iranians are targeted. We're not terrorist, there hasn't been a single terrorist from Iran," Ali said in a chat via Telegram on January 25.

U.S. officials have accused Iran of supporting the group behind the 1996 truck bombing of Khobar Towers in Saudi Arabia, which killed 19 U.S. servicemen. In 2013, the U.S. sentenced an Iranian-American man to 25 years in prison for his role in an Iranian plot to kill Saudi Arabia's ambassador to the United States.

Iran has been also accused by Argentinian authorities of involvement in the 1994 bombing of the Jewish center in Buenos Aires that killed 85 people and injured more than 300 others. Tehran denies the accusations.

Ali added that he hoped Trump would change his decision: "My dream is to study in America in order to have a better future, I hope this [ban] won't mean an end to my wish."

"Punishing Ordinary Iranians"

The United States is a leading destination for students from all over the world, with international student enrollment at public and private U.S. institutions totaling more than 1 million young people in 2015–16, according to the Institute of International Education, with roughly one-third of them coming from China and Iranians well outside the top 10 places of origin.

Hengameh, a mother of two in Tehran, told RFE/RL via Telegram she was offended by the U.S. decision. "I don't have plans to travel to America, but I know many who have relatives there. This will make things harder for them," she said, adding that obtaining a U.S. visa is already difficult for Iranians.

The United States and Iran cut off diplomatic ties decades ago, and Washington has relied on the Swiss government to represent its diplomatic interests in Iran ever since. As a result, to apply for a U.S. visa, Iranians already had to travel to a third country with a U.S. consulate for an interview and to pick up the actual document.

"This is discrimination, what have Iranians done to deserve this? We keep hearing that Iranians in [the U.S.] are among the most successful immigrants so what is the reason for this [ban]?" Hengameh asked.

Many Iranian-Americans emigrated to the United States in the period surrounding Iran's 1979 Islamic Revolution.

One possible consequence of a looming ban was highlighted by Dubai-based Reuters reporter Bozorgmehr Sharafedi, who wrote on Twitter that it would prevent his mother from visiting her son, his brother, in the United States.

Others expressed dismay that ordinary Iranians would be punished for actions by the Iranian establishment.

"Instead of targeting the regime, Trump is punishing the people," a reader commented on the Facebook page of RFE/RL's Radio Farda.

"Those who claim the U.S. doesn't have an issue with the Iranian people, only with the government, please pay attention," another reader wrote.

"The adoption of this [executive order] and similar laws will hurt only the Iranian people, and it won't have any impact on the travels of government [officials] to America," a comment on Radio Farda's Facebook page said.

"It's clear that [Trump] doesn't have a proper understanding of terrorists. Most of them are from Saudi Arabia, Pakistan, and other countries," another comment said.

Fifteen of the 19 hijackers who used passenger jets to carry out coordinated terrorist attacks against the United States on September 11, 2001, were from Saudi Arabia. Osama bin Laden, the leader of the Al-Qaeda terrorist network blamed for the attack, was a Saudi citizen.

One of the attackers in a mass shooting in San Bernardino, California, in 2015 was a Pakistani woman who grew up in Saudi

Arabia and was said to have been radicalized in part by sympathies for Islamic State (IS), a brutal militant Islamist group that controls parts of Iraq and Syria. Tashfeen Malik and her American-born husband of Pakistani descent, Rizwan Farook, killed 14 people and injured 22 others.

Quoting sources familiar with the visa process ahead of any official U.S. announcement, Reuters reported that Trump was likely to order the State Department to stop issuing visas to people from Syria, Iraq, Iran, Libya, Somalia, Sudan, and Yemen. He could also instruct U.S. Customs and Border Protection to stop any current visa holders from those countries from entering the United States.

VIEWPOINT 5

Trump's Travel Ban Has the Potential to Damage Science

John Morgan

In one last viewpoint looking at Trump's travel ban, John Morgan, politics and policy reporter for Times Higher Education, focuses specifically on the effect it would have on science. Morgan cites data showing many scientific partnerships between US and Iranian scientists. Interfering with these relationships by banning Iranians from entering the United States could not only inhibit the free exchange of ideas, but could do serious damage to science in both countries and have a worldwide negative effect on science, he argues. This piece was written after a US court blocked the first travel ban, but before Trump had replaced it with another (which was also blocked).

U S-Iran collaboration benefits the quality of research in both nations, according to data, while experts also warn that Donald Trump's attempted travel ban ignored the scientific, economic and security benefits to America from such links.

The strength of research ties and researcher mobility between the US and Iran—one of the countries targeted by the US president's attempted travel ban on entry for nationals from seven majority-Muslim nations via an executive order—is highlighted by figures from Elsevier's SciVal and Scopus databases.

With anti-immigration and anti-Muslim rhetoric being adopted by right-wing populist parties in a number of Western nations,

"Trump travel ban on Iranians 'would harm US science and nation,'" by John Morgan, Times Higher Education, February 20, 2017. Reprinted by Permission.

the potential for damage to a historically important scientific relationship such as that between the US and Iran is likely to concern universities around the world.

While Mr Trump abandoned attempts to overturn the legal block on his original executive order, he was due to unveil a new order this week. Seventeen of the most prestigious universities in the US, including Harvard, Yale and Stanford, had earlier filed legal papers seeking to join a lawsuit fighting the ban.

"By prohibiting persons from freely traveling to and from this country, the executive order divides students and their families, impairs the ability of American universities to draw the finest international talent, and inhibits the free exchange of ideas," the universities wrote in their legal submission.

The Elsevier data, shared with *THE*, shows that US academic relationships with Iran are by far the strongest of the seven nations targeted by the order. US researchers co-authored 8,821 papers with Iranian scientists between 2011 and 2015.

That makes Iran the US' 36th closest collaborator in research, narrowly behind the Republic of Ireland.

US-Iran co-authored papers had a field-weighted citation impact (widely regarded as an indicator of the quality of research) of 1.84. This compares with a citation impact of 1.46 for US-only authored papers and 0.84 for Iran-only authored papers. The world average is about 1.0.

Martin Edling Andersson, a senior product manager at Elsevier, said the fact the field-weighted citation impact for these US-Iran co-authored papers was higher "shows that both parties benefit".

Medicine, engineering and physics and astronomy are the main fields in which US and Iranian researchers collaborate.

By recording the location of authors' affiliated institutions, Elsevier's data also suggest that about 1,500 Iranian researchers active in publications have moved to the US long term since 1996.

The average field-weighted citation impact of these Iranian researchers who moved to the US is 1.93, well above the average for researchers who remain in Iran (0.88) and marginally above the average for researchers who do not leave the US (1.92).

Another 2,900 Iranian researchers were classed as "transitory" and spending most of their time in the US in that period, with an even higher average field-weighted citation impact of 2.21.

Jeroen Baas, head of data science at Elsevier, said that its analysis has established that, worldwide, there is a "very strong correlation between international collaboration and field-weighted citation impact. You see that the impact of publications that [are published through] an international collaboration is a lot higher."

And the ability of researchers to move around the world is a factor here.

"We've also seen that nations where there is a lot of mobility have a higher degree of international collaboration," said Dr Baas.

This suggests that were the US to limit entry to Iranian nationals, it could expect to lose out in the number of internationally co-authored papers it produces and thus in the quality of its research.

Prominent examples of Iranian researchers moving to the US include Stanford professor of mathematics Maryam Mirzakhani, who in 2014 became the first woman and first Iranian to win a Fields Medal, the world's most prestigious prize in mathematics. After an undergraduate degree at Sharif University of Technology in Tehran, she moved to the US to take a PhD at Harvard.

Another prominent Iranian-born scientist is Firouz Naderi, director for solar system exploration in Nasa's Jet Propulsion Laboratory, who studied in US higher education after being schooled in Iran.

According to figures from the US-based Institute of International Education, Iran was the 11th largest country of origin for international students enrolling at US universities and colleges in 2015–16. Iranian student enrollment increased by 8.2 per cent to 12,269, "the highest US enrollment by Iranians in 29 years", the IIE said in its 2016 *Open Doors* report. But this was still way below the peak flow of students from Iran, which was the top sender of international students to the US between 1974–75 and 1982–83, the IIE added.

After the Iranian Revolution in 1979 and the imprisoning of diplomats at its embassy in Tehran, the US severed diplomatic relations with Iran the following year. In 2015, Iran reached an agreement with six world powers—led by the US—in which it limited sensitive nuclear activities in exchange for the lifting of sanctions. However, the future of this agreement has been cast into doubt by the election of Mr Trump.

Alex Dehgan worked on developing a science diplomacy strategy with Iran under the Obama administration as senior adviser in the Office of the Special Adviser to the Secretary on the Gulf and Southwest Asia, within the US Department of State.

"Science and technology is a critical part of [Iran's] national strategy and even the national identity, and a source of great pride," said Iranian-born Dr Dehgan, a former chief scientist in the US Agency for International Development who is now a visiting senior fellow at Duke University and co-founder of Conservation X Labs.

While "there are many advantages to Iran for engagement with the United States…there are far more advantages for the US", he argued.

"US engagement with the Iranian scientific community builds an important connection to the country, and…creates a scaffolding on which an official relationship [between the nations] may be built…Such engagement transcends religion, race, and culture," Dr Dehgan said.

He added: "Science provides a common language and common values to engage Iranians in a manner that is transparent and non-threatening to the government, yet contains seeds for closer engagement and future change.

"The values inherent in science are US values, and include honesty, doubt, respect for evidence, transparency and openness, meritocracy, accountability and tolerance and, indeed, hunger for opposing points of view."

Engagement can also give a better picture of potential risks around Iran's "misuse of science" and prevent nuclear proliferation, Dr Dehgan argued.

He also pointed out that "many elements of the modern American lifestyle were created by Iranian-American immigrants," citing the roles of Iranian-Americans in founding tech companies ranging from Tinder (whose co-founder, Sean Rad, is the child of Iranian immigrants) to eBay (whose founder, Pierre Omidyar, is a French-Iranian-American).

"This is the wrong move for the United States," Dr Dehgan said of the attempted travel ban. "It is not who we are as a nation."

Iranians Are Pushing Back Against Their Government's Foreign Policy

Reese Erlich

While few Iranians are willing to openly criticize their government, many are beginning—quietly and "behind closed doors"—to question Tehran's foreign policy decisions. These dissenting voices are not limited to reformists, but include some conservatives as well. In this viewpoint from 2015, Reese Erlich, author, journalist, and expert on the Middle East, discusses Iran's practices regarding sectarianism and how those practices often differ from the nation's official policies. Erlich examines Iranian policy in key Middle Eastern countries, and says that Iranian citizens who are supporters of the Islamic government are beginning to question and call for change.

Iran's decision to sign the Vienna nuclear agreement has opened up a wide discussion on formerly taboo topics. For the first time in years, some Iranian intellectuals—both reformists and conservatives—are cautiously raising questions about Iran's foreign policy.

Some are criticizing previous government decisions related to the 1979 takeover of the US Embassy, duration of the Iran-Iraq War and high cost of Iran's nuclear program. Iran's support for Syria's President Bashar al-Assad is also up for discussion, according to Mohammad Pirali, managing editor of the conservative newspaper *Siasat-e Rooz* (Politics Daily). Iran provides the bulk of Assad's armaments, as well as military advisors.

"If Assad would have given people more political freedom, these matters would not have happened," he said, referring to

---

"Iranians quietly question their government's role in Syria and beyond," by Reese Erlich, Public Radio International, September 24, 2015. Reprinted by Permission.

the widespread rebellion against the Syrian government and subsequent civil war. Speaking of Assad's limited attempts to open a dialog with some opposition groups, Pirali said, "He's trying to open up politics now, but it's very late."

While some intellectuals are willing to speak openly, much of the criticism is made behind closed doors. Challenging the government on foreign policy can be dangerous, though military losses by a number of Iranian allies are emboldening more voices.

"Open criticism of Assad, Hezbollah or Hamas is forbidden," said Saeed Laylaz, a prominent reformist who was jailed for one year in 2009.

Iran and its allies have faced serious military setbacks in recent months. Sunni rebels in Syria have seized areas once controlled by Assad, who oversees a secular dictatorship that enjoys support from Alawites and Shia Muslims. In Iraq, the Islamic State continues to occupy areas once controlled by the pro-Iranian Iraqi government. And a Saudi-led war in Yemen has driven Iranian-backed rebels out of the country's second largest city, Aden.

Iran, a Shia-majority country that has forged strong alliances with Shia groups, sees itself as defending the oppressed in the Muslim world, whether Shia or Sunni. But Pirali admits that Iran faces major problems because of a perception that it only supports Shia movements. So Iran has unintentionally alienated Sunnis, according to Pirali.

"We should have supported all Muslims, all different branches," he said. "But we've supported groups that made others oppose us."

Officially, Iranian foreign policy doesn't support Shia against Sunni. Iran instead portrays itself as fighting US imperialism and Israeli aggression.

Of course Sunni and Shia have religious differences, says Mohammad Masjed Jamei, a former Iranian ambassador to the Vatican, who now teaches at the Foreign Ministry's School of International Relations. He compares Muslim doctrinal splits to those dividing Catholic and Orthodox Christians.

"The danger comes when people politicize the differences," he said. Iran does not promote sectarianism, he argues, but Saudi Arabia does. As the region's leading Sunni power, Saudi Arabia promulgates the Wahhabist interpretation of Islam, which demonizes Iran and all Shia.

"They claim that Iran wants to create a new empire, and Shia are not Muslims," said Masjed Jamei.

The US backs Saudi Arabia because of its oil wealth, Masjed Jamei said. From the 1950s through the 70s, the US used the Saudis to combat leftist and nationalist governments in the region. Then in the 1980s, the Saudis and the US backed ultra conservative mujahideen fighters, who ousted the Soviet Union from Afghanistan. The Saudis then spread Wahhabism throughout the Muslim world, which included support for al Qaeda in various countries, according to Masjed Jamei.

He argues that the US backed Wahhabism with no understanding of the long term implications. "The US accepted Saudi Arabia without researching the religious issues very well," he said.

While Saudi Arabia does indeed support extremist groups in Syria and elsewhere, Iran promotes its own brand of sectarianism as well.

Iran rallies supporters with calls for Shia to defend the faith. It justifies sending Iranian military advisors and Hezbollah troops to Iraq and Syria by claiming they are protecting religious shrines. Many ordinary Iranians see these wars in sectarian terms: Shia fighting Sunni.

And, as with the US troop deployments in the Middle East, Iran soon experienced mission creep. In Iraq the Iranians expanded their military presence in 2014 after the Islamic State captured Mosul and other areas. Iran threw support behind Shia militias, providing arms and training.

But loosely organized and undisciplined militias also attacked Sunni civilians. They kidnapped and murdered Sunnis suspected of ties with the Islamic State. Those attacks had serious political consequences, says the magazine editor Pirali.

"Wherever we supported only one group, it has ruined unity and brought instability," he said. Iran doesn't intentionally incite Shia against Sunni, he said, "but what we've done may have caused Sunnis to oppose us." He claims Iran is now in the process of fixing this error by supporting other Muslim groups.

But a close examination of Iranian policy in key countries calls that assertion into question:

Iraq

With the overthrow of Saddam Hussein's regime in 2003, the US got rid of one of Iran's worst enemies. Saddam had invaded Iran in 1980, and the two countries fought a bloody, eight-year war.

Iraq used chemical weapons against Iran.

Shia and Kurdish political parties that had opposed Saddam lived in exile in Iran for years. Their leaders later became members of parliament, prime minister and president. Iran continued economic, political and military support to those parties and their respective militias. Ironically, the US occupation produced a government more friendly to Iran than to the US.

In 2011 the US withdrew its troops from Iraq as agreed in the Status of Forces Agreement signed by President George W. Bush and the Iraqi government. Iran didn't want the Shia-dominated government to fall, according to Foad Izadi, an associate professor of world affairs at the University of Tehran.

"It looks like Iran was helping Shia," he said. "But in reality, that is not what Iran wanted to do." Continued fighting in Iraq doesn't help Iran, he argues. "Iran wants to make sure its neighbor is peaceful. Iran wants to sell a lot of goods and services to Iraq. You cannot do that when there's chaos."

Religious scholar Masjed Jamei adds that "Iran wants to protect shrines at Karbala and Najaf. Today there may be some Shia who kill Sunnis, but it was responding to attacks."

However, Sunnis in Iraq certainly don't view Iran that way. Many think that Iran controls the Baghdad government. Sunnis see Iran as helping their own sect, admits Professor Izadi. "The perception was exactly that."

Syria

Iran backs Assad in Syria's civil war for geopolitical, not religious reasons. Syria was the only Arab country to support Iran during the Iran-Iraq War. Assad joined Iran, Hezbollah and Hamas in opposing the 1993 Oslo Peace Accords between Israel and Palestine. Syria allows Iran to transport arms to Hezbollah across its border with Lebanon.

Bashar and his father Hafez al-Assad were secular dictators, and the Iranians never fully trusted them. For example, Ayatollah Khomeini never allowed Hafez al-Assad to visit Iran. But under present circumstances, Iran prefers Bashar al-Assad to a possible Sunni rebel victory.

Iran blames the US and Saudi Arabia for the rebellion against Assad, ignoring the initial popular movement that rose up against him. Seyed Mohammad Marandi, an associate professor of world studies at the University of Tehran, said some Iranians have soured on Assad. But most "believe they made the morally correct choice" in backing Assad's forces. "Despite all the problems, they are infinitely better than ISIL [the Islamic State] and al Qaeda."

But differences on Iran's Syria policy have occasionally surfaced. Ali Akbar Hashemi Rafsanjani, a former president of Iran and leading centrist politician, criticized Assad in unusually harsh terms two years ago.

In Syria, he said, "The prisons are crammed full and there is no more room, so they have seized a few stadiums to fill them up too. The Syrian people are experiencing harsh conditions. On the one hand, they are bombed with chemicals by their own government, and on the other hand, they can expect American bombs."

Yemen

In March of this year, Saudi Arabia launched a bombing campaign against Houthi rebels in Yemen, backed by some Sunni countries and the US. More recently, troops from the United Arab Emirates drove the rebels out of Aden and some neighboring areas. The Saudis argue they are fighting Iran's plans to dominate Yemen, even claiming Iran wants to conquer the Saudi holy cities of Mecca and Medina.

The rebel Houthi group, whose members are mostly from the Zaidi sect of Shia Islam, receive political support from Iran.

Mostafa Zahrani, director general of the Foreign Ministry's think tank, the Institute for Political and International Studies, says the support is not tied to the Houthis' religion.

"We decided to be on the side of the people," he said. "That's why we have influence. Millions support the Houthis." The Saudis accuse Iran of sending arms to the Houthis, a charge denied by Zahrani.

He argues that Iran's role is exaggerated by Saudi Arabia in order to justify their war. "Yemen has not been strategic for us," he said. "The war there has a long history, which doesn't have much to do with Iran in the first place."

But critics say Iran has the made the same mistakes in Yemen as elsewhere in the region. "We only supported Shia," noted magazine editor Pirali. "That's what brought the Sunnis against us."

Palestine

When accused of exclusively supporting Shia groups, Iranian officials point to their aid of the militant group Hamas in Palestine. As part of the "Axis of Resistance" fighting Israel, Iran provided political, economic and military support to Hamas, which is Sunni.

Hamas set up its political headquarters in Damascus in 2001 with backing from Syria and Iran. But relations soured since 2011 when Hamas sided with the popular uprising against Assad in Syria. Hamas began as the Palestinian offshoot of Egypt's Muslim

Brotherhood. It supported the Muslim Brotherhood of Syria in calls for the overthrow of Assad and holding elections, which the Syrian brotherhood may well have won.

In early 2012, Hamas leader Khaled Meshal left Damascus, and the group eventually moved its exile office to Doha, Qatar.

By 2015 Iran had cut off all aid to Hamas in Gaza, even as Palestinians suffered extreme hardship. Friction grew as Hamas sought to replace Iranian and Syrian support with aid from Arab gulf states and, most recently, Saudi Arabia.

Iran stepped up support for Islamic Jihad, a Sunni group that mostly operates in Gaza. One opinion poll showed Islamic Jihad had only 13 percent support among Palestinians. It is best known for periodically launching rockets from Gaza into Israel.

Iran has had difficulty explaining its relations with Hamas. At first it argued that Meshal didn't really represent Hamas' views on Syria. When other Hamas officials clearly expressed the same stand, Iran had to concede there is a major split between the two.

The country's leadership does not seem likely to change its foreign policy in the near future. But the willingness of some Iranians to publicly criticize aspects of that policy is an indication of deeper ferment.

Mehrdad Khadir, chief editor of the *Omid Javan* (Hope of the Youth) weekly magazine, says Iranians are now debating "three big questions" relating to key events after the 1979 Revolution:

- From 1979–80 Iranian students seized the US Embassy and held 52 American diplomats hostage. The crisis has disrupted US-Iran relations ever since. Khadir asked, "Why did they keep the US hostages for 444 days?"
- Iraq invaded Iran in 1980. But by June 1982 Iran had recaptured Iranian territory initially seized by Iraq. When the war ended in 1988, neither side has made any military gains, but Iran suffered many dead and wounded. "Why did the war last eight years?" asked Khadir.

- And more recently, Iran has spent tens of billions of dollars to develop its nuclear power program without every revealing the cost. "Why was there 10 years of nuclear power buildup, and how much did it cost?" asked Khadir.

Critics asking these questions consider themselves supporters of the 1979 Revolution and the Islamic government. They want to see meaningful change in that system. And they want to see an end to Iran's alienation from the Sunni Muslim world.

So far, however, they are only asking questions and raising mild criticisms. To fully answer them would require questioning the leadership of Supreme Leader Ali Khamenei, a red line few Iranians are willing to cross. A full reevaluation is not expected anytime soon.

Chronology

August 1953	A CIA-backed coup ousts Mohammed Mossadegh, the prime minister of Iran and replaces him with the U.S.-backed Shah.
March 1957	The United States and Iran sign a nuclear energy agreement calling for cooperation in peaceful uses of nuclear technology.
July 1968	Iran and the United States both sign the international Nuclear Nonproliferation Treaty.
May 1975	US president Gerald Ford signs a directive that will allow Iran to use American material to be made into fuel for its nuclear reactors.
December 1977	US president Jimmy Carter visits Iran and praises the Shah as a source of stability in Iran.
January 1979	An Islamic revolution in Iran overthrows the Shah and replaced him with the Ayatollah Khomeini, an exiled cleric.
February 1979	Khomeini returns to Iran. The US State Department evacuates more than 1,300 Americans.
November 4, 1979	Iranian militants storm the US Embassy in Tehran and take ninety people hostage, including sixty-six Americans.
November 14, 1979	President Carter freezes Iranian assets in US banks.

November 17, 1979	Khomeini orders the release of female and African American hostages, reducing the number of hostages to fifty-three.
April 1980	Carter cancels all diplomatic ties with Iran,and imposes additional sanctions.
April 1980	Carter stages a rescue attempt, but it is not successful.
July 1980	Another hostage is released, this one because of illness.
January 19, 1980	US secretary of state Warren Christopher negotiates a deal for the release of the remaining fifty-two hostages.
January 20, 1981	Immediately after the inauguration of a new US president (Ronald Reagan), the remaining hostages are released.
July 2, 1988	The United States accidentally shoots down an Iranian commercial airplane, killing 290 people.
June 1989	Ayatollah Khomeini dies in Iran.
February 1991	The United States turns down Iran's offer to mediate in the Persian Gulf War between the United States and Iraq.
August 1996	US president Bill Clinton imposes additional sanctions on Iran in response to Iran's financial support of terrorism.
August 2002	Secret nuclear facilities are discovered in Iran.
November 2004	Iran halts its nuclear weapons program.

August 2005 Secular conservative Mahmoud Ahmadinejad is elected president of Iran. Several former hostages claim Ahmadinejad was one of the captors, but a CIA investigation determined "with relative certainty" that he was not involved.

December 2006 The United Nations Security Council approves sanctions against Iran intended to curb its nuclear program.

2012 US and Iranian officials begin secret talks about Iran's nuclear program.

2013 Hassan Rouhani is elected president of Iran after promising to improve relations with the West. US president Barack Obama speaks with him by phone, the highest level of contact between the two nations in thirty years.

2015 Under the leadership of President Obama, Iran and six other nations agree to the provision of the JCPOA—also known as the Iran nuclear deal.

2016 Donald Trump is elected the forty-fifth president of the United States. By 2017, he adds new sanctions against Iran and begins trying to undo the Iran nuclear deal.

2017 President Hassan Rouhani is reelected in a landslide victory, representing a continuing commitment to political reform in Iran.

Bibliography

Books

Michael Axworthy. *Iran: What Everyone Needs to Know.* Oxford, UK: Oxford University Press, 2017.

James G. Blight, et al. *Becoming Enemies: Iran-US Relations and the Iran-Iraq War, 1979–1988.* Lanham, MD: Rowman and Littlefield, 2012.

David R. Collier. *Democracy and the Nature of American Influence in Iran, 1941–1979.* Syracuse, NY: Syracuse University Press, 2017.

Hamid Dabashi. *Iran, the Rebirth of a Nation.* New York, NY: Columbia University Press, 2016.

Richard Foltz. *Iran in World History.* Oxford, UK: Oxford University Press, 2016.

Mark Gasiorowski and Malcolm Byrne (eds). *Mohammad Mossaddeq and 1953 Coup in Iran.* Syracuse, NY: Syracuse University Press, 2004, 2017.

Yong Jui Lin, et al. *Iran.* (Cultures of the World). New York, NY: Cavendish Square, 2015.

Mahmood Monshipouri. *Inside the Islamic Republic: Social Change in Post-Khomeini Iran.* Oxford, UK: Oxford University Press, 2016.

Tamra B. Orr. *Iran and Nuclear Weapons.* New York, NY: Rosen, 2010.

David Oualaalou. *Volatile State: Iran in the Nuclear Age.* Bloomington, IN: Indiana University Press, 2018.

Misagh Parsa. *Democracy in Iran: Why It Failed and How It Might Succeed.* Cambridge, MA: Harvard University Press, 2016.

Trina Parsi. *Losing an Enemy: Obama, Iran, and the Triumph of Diplomacy*. New Haven, CT: Yale University Press, 2017.

Eugene Rogan. *The Fall of the Ottomans: The Great War in the Middle East*. New York, NY: Basic Books, 2016.

Amin Saikal (ed.). *The Arab World and Iran: A Turbulent Region in Transition*. Basingstoke, UK: Palgrave Macmillan, 2016.

Laura Secor. *Children of Paradise: The Struggle for the Soul of Iran*. New York, NY: Riverhead, 2017.

Periodicals and Internet Sources

BBC.Com, "US-Iran relations: A brief guide," BBC, November 24, 2014, http://www.bbc.com/news/world-middle -east-24316661

Saied Jafari, "Iran's efforts to improve ties with West 'fruitless' without US," *Al-Monitor*, October 12, 2015. http://www.al -monitor.com/pulse/originals/2015/10/iran-west-relations .html

Molly McCluskey, "Trump's proposed Muslim ban complicates US-Iranian relations," *Middle East Eye*, January 26, 2017. http://www.middleeasteye.net/news/trump-s-proposed -muslim-ban-complicates-iranian-relations-1146418901

Ambassador Seyed Hossein Mousavian, "Future of US-Iran Relations," Al Jazeera Media Network, April 6, 2014. http:// studies.aljazeera.net/en /dossiers/2014/03/201433111714876246.html

Garrett Nada, "If sanctions are lifted, here's what trade between Iran and the US could look like," Quartz, April 24, 2015. https://qz.com/390121/if-sanctioned-are-lifted-heres-what -trade-between-iran-and-the-us-would-look-like

Websites

American Iranian Council (www.us-iran.org)

The AIC's goal is to be a catalyst for positive change in the relationship between the United States and Iran—bringing the countries together by promoting truth, understanding, and dialogue. Founded in 1990, the AIC focuses on public policy, which they hope to influence through research, education, and mobilization.

Iran-United States Claims Tribunal (www.iusct.net)

Established in January 1981, the Iran-United States Claims Tribunal seeks to resolve certain claims by nationals of one state party against the other state party and certain claims between the state parties. The tribunal consists of nine members, three appointed by each government and three third-country members appointed by the other six.

Iranian-American Political Action Committee (www.iranianamericanpac.org)

IAPAC is the registered bipartisan political action committee of the Public Affairs Alliance of Iranian Americans (PAAIA). IAPAC supports candidates for public office attuned to the concerns of the Iranian American community and also supports and encourages Iranian Americans to actively participate in the US democratic process and run for public office.

The National Iranian American Council (www.niacouncil.org)

The NIAC is a nonpartisan, nonprofit organization dedicated to strengthening the voice of Iranian Americans and promoting greater understanding between the American and Iranian people. They accomplish their mission through expert research and analysis, civic and policy education, and community building.

Organization of Iranian American Communities-U.S. (www.oiac-us.com)

The OIAC works toward a democratic, secular, and nonnuclear government in Iran, founded on the respect for human rights, gender equality, religious and ethnic tolerance, as well as social and economic justice and security for America.

Index

A

Abbas, Shabbir, 118
Abdi, Ali, 111, 112
Ahmadinejad, Mahmoud, 19, 31, 32, 34, 56, 57, 59, 60, 63, 68, 70–71, 108
protest against, 60
American Israel Public Affairs Committee (AIPAC), 99, 100
Anglo-Persian (Iranian) Oil Company, 20, 21, 22, 24, 49
Arab-Israeli War, 26, 46
Assad, Bashar al-, 56, 70, 130–131, 134, 135, 136
Ayatollah, as leader of Iran, 13, 25

B

ballistic missile test, of Iran, 81–82, 83, 84–85, 107
Baskerville, Howard C., 34, 35
Braml, Josef, 63, 64
breakout, 73–75
estimating timing for, 78–80
times for, 72, 73, 78
Brimmer, Esther D., 116

Bush, George H. W., 29–30
Bush, George W., 30–31, 32, 34, 46, 48, 52, 62–63, 133
Bushehr nuclear complex, 31, 34

C

Carter, Jimmy, 27, 28–29, 49, 50
Central Intelligence Agency (CIA), 22, 23, 24, 28, 36–37, 38, 41, 44, 49, 84
centrifuges
advanced, 76–78, 79
Iranian operation of, 69–70, 72, 74–75, 80, 88, 99
clerics, 13, 14, 25, 61
Clinton, Bill, 30–31, 46, 51, 93
Cold War, 21–24, 25, 30–32, 37, 41
communism, 18, 23, 24, 25, 40
corruption, 14, 49–50, 57, 94

D

Dehgan, Alex, 128, 129
dissent, in Iran, 14, 41, 130
Dworkin, Anthony, 60–61, 63

E

Eisenhower, Dwight, 22, 23, 24, 41, 48–49

G

Green Revolution, 34

H

Hamas, 31, 46, 52, 131, 134, 135–136
Hartle, Terry W., 115
Hezbollah, 19, 29, 46, 51, 52, 70, 131, 132, 134
Hossein Ali Montazeri, Ayatollah, 61
hostage crisis, 13, 17, 28–29, 30, 32, 45, 46, 50, 56, 136
  consequences of, 59–61, 63–64
  moving beyond, 50–51
Houthis, 103, 107, 135
Huntington, Samuel, 30
Hussein, Saddam, 29, 31
  invasion of Kuwait, 29–30
  overthrow of, 133

I

inflation, 26, 57, 62
International Atomic Energy Agency (IAEA), 69, 76, 77, 82, 89, 99, 107

Iran-Iraq War, 29, 45, 92, 93, 130, 134
Iran-Contra Affair, 29, 51
Iranian National Oil Company, 92, 93
Islamic Republic
  economy of, 57
  formation of, 13, 27–28
  politics under, 62, 68
  push for reform in, 55–56
  relations with the United States, 29, 31, 52, 59, 60
Islamic State, 104, 123–124, 131, 132–133, 134
Israel, 24, 31, 34, 42, 46, 52, 57, 59, 66, 67, 68, 70, 71, 97, 107, 135, 136
  aggression of, 131
  influence of, 99–100, 102–103

J

Jafari, Payam, 113, 114
Jenkins, Reverend John I., 117
Johnson, Lyndon B., 25, 26
Joint Comprehensive Plan of Action (JCPOA), 17, 81–82, 84–85. *See also* nuclear deal

K

Kennedy, John F., 25, 44
Khadir, Mehrdad, 136, 137

sectarianism, 130, 132

Shah, as leader of Iran, 12–13, 19–20, 21, 22, 23–24, 25, 26, 28, 38–39, 40, 41–42, 43–44, 45, 71

relationship with the United States, 24, 45, 48, 50

repressiveness of, 24–25, 27

Shia Islam, 31, 70, 71, 131, 132, 133, 135

Soltan, Neda Agha, 32, 34

Stalin, Josef, 20–21

Status of Forces bills, 43, 45, 133

Sunni Islam, 70, 131, 132–133, 134, 135, 136, 137

T

Tajzadeh, Mostafa, 55

terrorism, 13–14, 30, 66, 70, 85, 112, 113, 120, 122, 123

allegations of President Bush against Iran, 31

of Hezbollah, 51

Iranian support of, 52, 121

three pillars, of revolutionary ideology, 57

Truman, Harry S., 21, 22, 40, 41, 48

Trump, Donald, 13, 14, 81–82, 85, 97, 104, 107, 116–117

Muslim travel ban of, 97, 105–106, 110–119, 120–124, 125–129, 117

position on Iran, 104, 107, 108

Tudeh Party, 21, 23–24

U

uranium, Iranian enriched, 31, 69–70, 72, 74–75, 76–78, 79

W

White Revolution, 25, 26

World War II, 21, 36, 38, 39–40

Z

Zahedi, Fazlollah, 22, 23–24

Zahrani, Mostafa, 135

Zinouri, Nazanin, 114